£3.95

THE REAR COLUMN
and other plays

First seen in London at the Globe Theatre in February 1978 in a production directed by Harold Pinter, *The Rear Column* is based on a historical incident in the Congo in the 1880's. A small group of officers, stranded in the middle of Africa with dwindling supplies, come to realise that they are in the hands of a Commanding Officer who is more than a little round the bend.

The Rear Column and also *Molly*, the second play in this volume, are surprisingly different in treatment from the earlier plays — *Butley*, *Otherwise Engaged* and *Dog Days* — and mark a new departure for Simon Gray as a writer.

Molly, based on the Alma Rattenbury case in the thirties, was chosen to open the New Spoleto Festival at Charleston in May 1977, where it was extremely well received:

 'A highly charged, powerful play' *Wall Street Journal*

 'Molly is quite unlike any play that Simon Gray has written . . . a signal change of direction that reveals fresh beginnings and new horizons.' *Time Magazine*

Molly was first seen in Britain at the Watford Palace Theatre in November 1977. The Times critic described the play as:

 '. . . this crisply written . . . farcical tragedy . . . unerringly funny all the way through' and pointed out '. . . the withdrawal and complexities familiar in Gray's work and far subtl the ethical clichés his critics have tended to

John Barber, reviewing the play in the

 '. . . throughout the writing is warn uncompromising.'

The third play in the volume, *Man in a* the BBC, concerns the breakdown of a n ssful woman novelist and her ineffectual husba ay malicious cat and mouse games with the unwilling participation of a third party — the man in the side-car.

UNIVERSITY OF WINNIPEG
LIBRARY
DISCARDED
515 Portage Avenue
Winnipeg, Manitoba R3B 2E9

by the same author

Plays

Sleeping Dog (published by Faber)
Wise Child (published by Faber)
Dutch Uncle (published by Faber)
Spoiled (published by Eyre Methuen)
The Idiot (published by Eyre Methuen)
Butley (published by Eyre Methuen)
Otherwise Engaged,
Two Sundays *and*
Plaintiffs and Defendants
(published by Eyre Methuen)
Dog Days (published by Eyre Methuen)

Novels

Colmain (published by Faber)
Little Portia (published by Faber)
Simple People (published by Faber)
A Comeback for Stark (under the pseudonym
Hamish Reade, published by Faber)

On the front cover the photograph of Major E. M. Barttelot was reproduced from The Life of Edmund Musgrave Barttelot *by Walter George Barttelot (Richard Bentley & Son, 1890) and the photographs of J. Rose Troup, J. S. Jameson, H. Ward, W. Bonny and Tippu Tib from* With Stanley's Rear Column *by J. Rose Troup (Chapman & Hall Ltd, 1890). The photograph on the back cover is reproduced by courtesy of Beryl Gray.*

UNIVERSITY OF WINNIPEG
LIBRARY
515 Portage Avenue
Winnipeg, Manitoba R3B 2E9

PR
6057
·R33 R4
1978

Simon Gray

THE REAR COLUMN
and other plays

EYRE METHUEN . LONDON

First published in 1978 by Eyre Methuen Ltd
11 New Fetter Lane, London EC4P 4EE
Copyright © 1978 by Simon Gray
Printed in Great Britain by Whitstable Litho Ltd
Whitstable, Kent

ISBN 0 413 39160 4 (Hardback)
ISBN 0 413 39170 1 (Paperback)

All rights whatsoever in this play are strictly reserved and
application for performance etc should be made before
rehearsal to Judy Daish, 16 Cadogan Lane, London S.W.1. No
performance may be given unless a licence has been
obtained.

This paperback edition is sold subject to the condition that it
shall not, by way of trade or otherwise, be lent, resold, hired
out, or otherwise circulated without the publisher's prior
consent in any form of binding or cover other than that in
which it is published and without a similar condition including
this condition being imposed on the subsequent purchaser.

CONTENTS

This book is dedicated to the memory of Clive Goodwin, to whom I owe more than I can say.

S.G.

THE REAR
COLUMN

Author's Note

I had a purple patch between March 1969 and February 1971
when I managed three flops in a row. *Dutch Uncle,* produced by
the Royal Shakespeare Company, was a farce that depressed its
audiences, appalled the reviewers (one of whom based on it his
entire case for bringing booing back to the theatre) and shamed
myself and my loved ones: a clear example I think of a flop
total; then came an adaptation of *The Idiot*, which didn't do as
badly by its audiences, but was so comprehensively done over by
reviewers anxious to establish their Dostoievsky credentials that
the National Theatre, which during rehearslas and previews had
predicted great success, withdrew the play from its repertory
more quickly than it decently could. This flop d'estime was
followed by *Spoiled*, which though well enough received by the
reviewers (apart from a fellow-failure of a dramatist who
seized the opportunity to upgrade himself by saluting me as the
worst playwright in England), ran for three weeks to a handful of
agrophiles at the Haymarket, and was a flop merely.

I seem in retrospect to have spent most of this period with my
head down, to conceal as I went about my daily business cheeks
that flamed easily and eyes that watered over trifles. The only
glimmer of compensation came from my old friend and sticker-
by Tony Gould, who over a long lunch in a Chinese restaurant
(probably) told me the story of Stanley's march to the relief of
Emin Pasha, and more particularly the fate of his rear
column, left behind in the encampment of Yambuya, by the
banks of the Arruwimi River, in the Year of Grace 1887. There
were times during the working years that followed when,
stuck in some Yambuya of my own making, with five characters
I could neither completely abandon nor conduct to their final
destinies, I regretted the lunch more than the flops from which it
had promised redemption. In the worst patches I turned away to
write other stage plays — *Butley, Otherwise Engaged, Dog Days*
and *Molly*; and two television plays — *Plaintiffs and Defendants*

and *Two Sundays* — but in between I always, for shorter or longer periods, returned to Yambuya: and a few months ago, some seven years after I first heard the story, got Mr Stanley to come back at last, and bring a painful relief to us all.

7th December, 1977

At the time of going to press THE REAR COLUMN was
scheduled to be presented by Michael Codron at the Globe
Theatre, London, on 22 February 1978 with the following cast:

BONNY	Donald Gee
JAMESON	Jeremy Irons
WARD	Simon Ward
TROUP	Clive Francis
BARTTELOT	Barry Foster
STANLEY	Michael Forrest
JOHN HENRY	Riba Ackabusi
NATIVE WOMAN	Dorrett Thompson

Directed by Harold Pinter
Designed by Eileen Diss
Lighting by Nick Chelton

Act One

Scene One

A large store room in the Yambuya Camp, on the banks of the Arruwimi River, the Congo. It is June, 1887. Late afternoon.

There are boxes back left and back right of stage. Between them, back stage centre, large double doors. A canvas flap, stage right. A large table, centre stage. Some travelling chests which also serve as chairs. Stage left, a travelling desk and a chair, a settee.

The double doors are partly open, to let in light. There are two turtles, attached by lengths of string to the table legs.

BONNY is studying the room, clearly having just entered it for the first time. He goes to the work desk, gives something on it a cursory, rather contemptuous glance, goes over to the table, lets out an exclamation, picks up a turtle, then the other one. Puts them on the table.

JAMESON (*enters through flap*). Oh, Mr Bonny — you've met Herman and King, I see.

BONNY. Oh. I was hoping I'd met some soup.

JAMESON (*laughs*). One evening, no doubt. But one needs time to prepare.

BONNY. It doesn't take long to boil up a pair of turtles, does it?

JAMESON. I meant for the loss.

BONNY. What, they're pets, are they?

JAMESON. Well, they've kept the Major and myself company through some pretty lonely times. When he was ill, they were all I had to talk to, and when I was ill I used to imagine the three of them passing riotous evenings together. I got them from one of the village chiefs on my first trip out after Stanley's departure. He assumed I was a slaver, come to steal

his wife and ransom her for food. He offered me these before I
could put him straight — I couldn't speak much of the lingo
then.

BONNY. What was the wife like?

JAMESON. I didn't see her, but I'm sure she wouldn't have
made into soup.

BONNY. No, but she might have done for a pet. Then when you'd
finished with her, you could have traded her in for the soup.

JAMESON (*laughs politely*). This one's Herman because he reminds
me of a German Professor of Zoology under whom I once
studied, and this is King because he reminded the Major of the
horse on which he was taught to ride, as a child in Sussex. Two
patient, comforting, slow-witted fellows from our past, whose
own pasts go far further back than ours. If you look at Herman's
markings, you'll see he must be nearly a hundred.

BONNY. Oh. (*He looks quickly, without interest.*)

JAMESON. While King is a mere stripling of some six decades. I'm
sorry to ramble on. One's got out of the habit of succinctness
these last two months. Where are your two companions, by
the way?

BONNY. Troup's dealing with his Soudanese, and Ward with his
Zanzibaris.

JAMESON. You've got your men down already have you, good.

BONNY. Oh, I didn't have charge of any men — as I'm the one with
medical training Mr Stanley made me responsible for the mules.

JAMESON. Did they give you a bad time?

BONNY. Let's say we only understood each other when I was
having them fed.

JAMESON. In that respect, they don't seem too unlike the
men.

BONNY. A bit unlike your men, in that they were at least fed. I
took a stroll around the compound after I'd done with the
brutes. You're in a bad way here, aren't you? A very bad way.
(*Pause.*) How many have you lost?

JAMESON. Nineteen Zanzibaris, twelve Soudanese.

BONNY. Well, you'll lose a few more tonight. Fever, ulcers on
the back and legs — malnutrition, in other words. What have
the poor devils been eating?

JAMESON. Much the same as the Major and myself. The odd
fish they buy from the natives, or a goat, sometimes a fowl.
But the staple diet is the manioc root. For the Soudanese,
that is. The Zanzibaris won't eat meat, so for them it's
manioc and more manioc. Of course they won't cook it
properly. The manioc has to be boiled slowly and then drained.
They toss it into the pot then swallow it straight down. It
frequently swells in their stomachs . . .

WARD *enters.*

The Major and I have given at least twenty cooking
demonstrations between us. But they pay no attention.

BONNY. Was it like this when Mr Stanley was here?

JAMESON. Perhaps the Soudanese had a little more meat, and
the Zanzibaris a little more fish, as Mr Stanley is famously
clever at trading with the natives. But some of the
Zanzibaris had begun to die before he left.

WARD. In other words, you've been having a rather grim time.

JAMESON. It's not particularly pleasant to watch men dying.
They seem, the Zanzibaris especially, to settle into death
before they become properly ill — as if death itself were the
disease. They lie in their own dung waiting — the flies come
up — well, you've seen and smelt for yourselves. At first we
tried to keep them on the move, our policy was work and
more work, but once we'd built the palisades and fenced
ourselves in there was no work, to speak of. We can't let
them out except in small details to gather wood, and even
then they try to quarrel with the natives or what's worse
trade them their guns for food. And as we'd rather be
surrounded by natives who are reasonably friendly and
unarmed . . . So we're left with the camp routine, and that's
not adequate. These men are porters by nature, used to
marching for long periods and to camping for short ones.

WARD. So the fact of it is, they're dying of hunger and
boredom.

JAMESON. In a sense, Mr Ward. Though it doesn't quite
catch the feeling of the two months they've spent doing it in.

WARD. And how many have died of a flogging?

JAMESON (*after a pause*). One.

WARD. But there's been more than one flogging, I take it? I
saw a creature out there whose back was in ribbons.

JAMESON. There have been several floggings, Mr Ward. Once
they'd realized they could get a chicken or some fish or
even a goat for their rifles, and once they'd started thieving —
the Major began by issuing warnings, and when they didn't
take was forced to back them up with floggings.

WARD. Which doubtless haven't taken either.

JAMESON. An old debate, Mr Ward. We have no way of knowing,
have we? how many we've deterred. We only know how many
haven't been. You blame us for it, then?

WARD. Good God, no. Once you start, you have to go on, and
nobody's yet discovered an alternative to starting. I can't really
see that there's anything here to surprise. Constant sickness
punctuated by regular floggings — the inevitable conditions of
a large, stationary camp in the Congo. The only solution is to get
moving as quickly as possible.

JAMESON. Amen to that!

TROUP (*enters*). It appears I'm not to get one after all, can you
believe it? It's not enough that we find Stanley gone in spite of
his reassurances that he'd wait on us, it's not enough that we
were misled on that, but it turns out that after weeks of hard
travelling by day and the utmost misery and discomfort at
night, I'm still to be deprived — what the devil am I to do?

WARD. Mr Troup is talking of a bed, Mr Jameson.

JAMESON. A bed? But weren't you issued with a bed in London?

TROUP. Oh yes, Mr Jameson, I was issued with one, and here's my
chit to prove it — you see, it entitles me to one bed at the
expedition's expense. When I met with Mr Stanley at the Falls,
I presented him with this chit, signed by Mr MacKinnon of the
Committee, and he said that as all the beds were packed in the
steamer, I'd have to wait until we met up here. Well, here I
am, and here's my chit, but as there's no Stanley, there's no
bed. (*He laughs bitterly*.) Anyway, that'll teach me a little
savvy. I saw a bed lying free on the wharf at the Falls, but I
refrained from taking it. And what happened? Old Ward here took
it instead. He was quite right, by God, if I'd known the plight
my scruples were to land me in, I'd have fought him for it, I
would you know, Ward!

WARD. Yes, old chap, I know, but look, there must be a spare bed
somewhere in the Camp, there always is.

TROUP. Oh yes, three. Three spare beds. But according to the

Major, they belong to Mr Stanley, and are on no account to be touched. According to the Major. Though why the devil he thinks Stanley would object —

JAMESON. Mr Troup, I think I can help you. Mr Parke brought up an extra bed for Jephson, who fortunately brought his own. Parke asked me to add it to the loads for him, but he and I are good friends, I'm sure he wouldn't mind my letting you have the use of it.

TROUP. What? You mean there is a bed — I shall have a bed — tonight, you mean?

JAMESON. This very minute, if you like.

TROUP. No, no, it's just that — (*laughs*) after sleeping on wet grass between damp blankets — or propped against trees — I can hardly grasp — it's uncommonly kind of you, Mr Jameson, thank you.

BARTTELOT (*enters, through the flap, carrying a wooden stick with a metal tip*). Ah, Mr Troup, Mr Ward, here you are, I've been looking for you, and Mr Bonny. We must be careful that your Soudanese, Mr Troup, and your Zanzibaris, Mr Ward, are kept separate from those already in the camp. We've had a bout of sickness, as you've probably noticed, and there's no point the fresh men being contaminated. We'll have to put guards on them or they'll drift — they'll drift — and Mr Bonny, your mules, a guard on those too, if you please. Mule meat is something of a delicacy with the Soudanese — with Mr Jameson and myself, come to think of it, eh Jamie? (*He laughs.*) Well gentlemen, by this time you'll have some idea of our situation. I've no doubt you're as disappointed to find Mr Stanley gone as Mr Jameson and I were when we were left behind to wait for you. But he was anxious to make all possible speed to Emin Pasha, and pull him out before the Mahdi gets to him and with luck we'll either catch him up or not be too far behind him.

BONNY. As I understand it, we have to wait on for more porters.

BARTTELOT. Yes, Mr Bonny, another six hundred. We have nine hundred loads, each one of which Mr Stanley believes essential — food, quinine, rifles — and including the ones you've brought up just over three hundred porters. So we can't move until we have the other six hundred.

TROUP. Where are they going to come from? As Bonny, Ward and I were the only officers left behind —

BARTTELOT. They're being brought up by Tippu-Tib.

WARD. Tippu-Tib!

BARTTELOT. That's right, Mr Ward. Tippu-Tib. He and Mr Stanley came to an arrangement here before Stanley set out.

BONNY. Who is Tippu-Tib?

WARD. He's an Arab slave trader. Half Arab that is, and half Manyema. Which makes him wholly abominable.

BARTTELOT. But a particular friend of Mr Stanley's. You know him then?

WARD. By reputation, of course. No one who's spent any time in this part of the Congo could fail to. And I've come across his auxiliaries, who usually turn out to be his relatives as well. I've also come across his victims. I met poor Deane at Stanley Falls a year ago, just after the Arabs had burnt him out.

JAMESON. But on that occasion Tippu-Tib wasn't the Arab responsible.

WARD. Oh, Tippu is always the Arab responsible. This country is really his bazaar, you see, and the people in it his merchandise, and every Arab a relative, and every relative an agent.

BARTTELOT. Nevertheless, as I said, he and Mr Stanley are the greatest of friends.

WARD. They both choose their friends wisely.

JAMESON. And they have an agreement for the porters.

BONNY. When is he expected then, Major, with the porters?

BARTTELOT. Mr Stanley couldn't be precise. But he was hoping they'd arrive shortly after you.

BONNY. Any day now then.

WARD. Did you yourselves take part in these arrangements with Tippu-Tib?

BARTTELOT. No, Mr Stanley and Tippu-Tib kept themselves to themselves during the time the Arabs were in the Camp. None of the other officers had the pleasure of being introduced to him either, he has an aversion to any shows of white strength, apparently, we scarcely got a glimpse of him.

TROUP. And this is the man we're to wait for! An Arab slaver who distrusts white men —

JAMESON. He doesn't distrust Mr Stanley.

BONNY. Have you heard anything of him since he left?

JAMESON. Oh, just rumours. A few weeks ago the natives were full of talk of Arabs, I went over to explore but couldn't find any trace — the natives have a particular interest in Arabs, of course, they fear them as slavers but desire them as food.

TROUP. Food!

JAMESON. They believe they can take their cunning into their own systems, by eating them.

TROUP. But look here — do you mean to say — I thought cannibalism had been wiped out in these parts, by Stanley himself when he was here before. There was a long report in *The Times*, only last year —

WARD. The local chiefs probably haven't received their copies yet.

JAMESON (*laughs*). The problem is, Mr Troup, that it's hard to wipe out an appetite. Mr Stanley made the chiefs promise to stop gobbling each other up —   .

WARD. As he made the slavers promise to give up slaving. A promise in the jungle may become a fact in London, but you don't believe that Tippu-Tib is going to hire our six hundred men, do you? Or that Stanley believes he is.

TROUP. But good God — good God — Stanley told us nothing of this sort of thing in London. We signed on to march direct to the relief of Emin Pasha — and instead here we are hanging about waiting for some brigand of an Arab to enslave some porters —

BARTTELOT. While outside there are cannibals and inside three hundred hungry and contagious niggers. Exactly, Mr Troup. That is our situation, and will remain our situation until Tippu-Tib arrives to release us from it.

WARD. What is Mr Stanley's alternative proposal?

BARTTELOT. Alternative to what?

WARD. In the event of Tippu's not turning up shortly. He's notorious for a number of things, but not for his punctuality. At least I've never heard of it.

BARTTELOT. There is no alternative.

WARD. But in the event of his not turning up at all.

BARTTELOT. There is still no alternative. Mr Stanley will accept no alternative to the safety of his loads. He is clear that he expects them and must have them. There is no alternative, Mr Ward. Tippu-Tib must turn up. And until he does we shall have to make the best of it.

WARD. But surely — (*He stops.*)

JAMESON. You'll be wanting to settle into your quarters — there's a shower behind my tent. The water comes up from the Arruwimi, it's dirty, warm and it smells, I'm afraid, but it's wet.

BARTTELOT. We've been in the habit of eating at sun-down, if that suits you. We've kept a goat specially for this occasion — though we've been tempted by it often enough, haven't we, Jamie? — so at least this first night you'll have meat rather than manioc. By the way, an unnecessary warning, I'm sure, but anything you have in the way of provisions should be kept locked in your trunks — they're not above trying to slip into the tents, we caught one just the other day — and your rifles, goes without saying.

WARD. Actually, Major, I've no provisions whatsoever. So I'd be very glad to have what's coming to me as soon as you can manage it.

BONNY. Yes, I'm right out of tea.

BARTTELOT. I'm sorry, Mr Ward. There's nothing coming to you that I know of.

TROUP. Six months provisions, guaranteed by the Committee.

WARD. To be provided when we got our men up here.

BARTTELOT. I know nothing about it.

TROUP. But they must surely have been left behind by Mr Stanley.

BARTTELOT. Very possibly. But as Mr Stanley left no instructions on the matter, there's no way of knowing.

TROUP. But what about you and Jameson? Have you had yours?

BARTTELOT. Mr Stanley did give some out before he left, yes. But he left me no authorisation to give you any.

TROUP. My authorisation comes from the Committee in London.

BARTTELOT. Then perhaps you should take it up with the Committee in London.

WARD. Personally I shan't be needing jungle provisions in London, at least as long as there are still shops and restaurants there. Anyway, my chit is signed personally by Mr Stanley.

BARTTELOT. Then it's to Mr Stanley you must apply, when we catch up with him.

TROUP. We need our provisions now, sir.

BARTTELOT. I can't help you, sir.

TROUP. But you can, sir. They must be here, among the loads Mr Stanley left behind.

BARTTELOT. As Mr Stanley didn't say, how can you know that?

WARD. Ratiocination, possibly. In that if Mr Stanley owes us some provisions, which he does; and has left behind a large number of loads, which he has; and arranged for us to wait here with you, to help bring up those loads, which he did; then he's scarcely likely to have taken our provisions on with him; which one can therefore conclude he hasn't.

BARTTELOT. Are you making fun of me, sir!

WARD. No, Major. I was simply helping you to a conclusion.

BARTTELOT. Well, one may conclude anything with Mr Stanley, as a sure way of ending up in the wrong for it. But one thing one can be sure about, in the matter of Mr Stanley's intentions, is that his instructions are to be carried out to the very letter, and only to the very letter, however inconvenient that may be to the rest of the world. Mr Jameson will confirm that as Commanding Officer of this Rear Column, I must do as Mr Stanley said, but I may on no account do what I think he might have said, had he been here to say it. Isn't that so, Mr Jameson? I sympathise with you, of course, and if my Commanding Officer weren't Mr Stanley, you'd find your Commanding Officer a very much more obliging fellow, believe me.

TROUP. Do you mean to say that we're not to have our provisions simply because Stanley forgot to include them in his instructions.

BARTTELOT. But we cannot say that he forgot. He may well have remembered not to include them.

TROUP. And why should he do that?

BARTTELOT. Because — because — I don't know, how should I?

TROUP. This is nonsense, nonsense! You tell us we're not to have provisions which we were guaranteed as members of this expedition, provisions that do not belong personally to Mr Stanley, because in your view Mr Stanley is some sort of — some sort of — punctilious lunatic. Well sir, let me remind you that I have had dealings with Mr Stanley, and a saner and more practical man I've never met. Sir, I believe you're making us the victims of some private misunderstanding between Mr Stanley and yourself.

BARTTELOT. Have no fear of that, sir, there's no misunderstanding at all between Mr Stanley and myself. I understand him only too well. Certainly too well to allow myself to be the victim of your misfortune. He wouldn't hesitate to use this opportunity to ruin my career, my reputation at home —

WARD (*after a pause*). Stanley will ruin your career and your reputation if you furnish us with provisions that are rightly ours?

BARTTELOT. Ask Mr Jameson if I'm over-stating the case?

JAMESON. The Major has reason to be careful, where Mr Stanley's orders are in question. Mr Stanley on an expedition is a very different man from Mr Stanley on the Falls or sitting with Mr MacKinnon on the Committee in London. Jephson, Parke, Stairs — all the officers who've gone on with him would concur.

BARTTELOT. And it is through his orders, some of them impossible to perform, that he gets at us. He's as savage with initiative as he is with inefficiency. Well, he'll not get at me, sir, not any more. And I'm sorry if others must suffer for it.

TROUP. Can we see these orders, Major? As we're to be so strictly governed by them?

BARTTELOT (*after a pause, during which he stares at* TROUP). You would have seen them in due course, Mr Troup, whether you'd requested to or not.

TROUP (*reads them through quickly*). There's very little to them, and what there is can scarcely be said to have been written in a spirit of animosity. (*Passing them to* WARD.) Rather the reverse.

BARTTELOT. He knew that I would not be the only one to read them.

TROUP. I see he expressly requests you to take Mr Ward's, Mr
  Bonny's and my advice — along with Mr Jameson's.

BARTTELOT. No, Mr Troup, he tells me to ask you for your advice,
  not take it. The responsibility remains entirely mine. It's in the
  same sentence — heed their advice while being solely answerable
  for the decisions. At a first reading you will fail to detect, as Mr
  Jameson and I failed to detect, the real subtlety of what he's
  written. Or notice a major anomaly.

WARD. I certainly can't find an anomaly — or even much in the
  way of subtlety. It's all most emphatic, down to the number of
  brass-rods we're to pay to the porters per day.

BARTTELOT. The brass-rods — oh yes — he'd be emphatic about
  the brass-rods. He knows the value of a brass-rod in the Congo
  as a Jew knows a sovereign in Kensington.

JAMESON. But apart from the brass-rods he is emphatic. But
  without being precise.

BARTTELOT. Exactly. Exactly. And look — see what he says
  about the palisade.

WARD (*looks*). Merely that you're to build one. Which you
  have — an admirable one. What could be more sensible?

BARTTELOT. Ah, but what follows the order — (*He recites.*) For
  remember, it is not the natives alone who may wish to assail
  you, but the Arabs and their followers may, through some cause
  or other, quarrel with you and assail the camp.

WARD. Well?

BARTTELOT. Well, Mr Ward, you yourself have confirmed our
  worst suspicions. By Arabs whom can he mean but Tippu-Tib.
  So Stanley has gone out of his way to warn us against a man
  he claims as his friend, on whom he has made us depend,
  without whose arrival we cannot move!

WARD. But good God, of course he'd warn you! He knows better
  than anyone — friend or not, Tippu-Tib is a very dangerous man.
  But he also knows that Tippu is the only man in the Congo who
  could raise six hundred porters, by whatever means. Tippu is
  both totally indispensable and completely untrustworthy. That
  is the nature of the beast!

JAMESON. But as you've pointed out, he leaves us with no
  alternative.

WARD. And as Major Barttelot pointed out — with considerable force — there is no alternative. If the loads are essential, then the porters are essential. If the porters are essential —

TROUP. So is this Tippu-Tib. Exactly! I must say (*laughs*) if this is all!

BARTTELOT. It isn't all! Or rather it is all — and that's the damned subtlety of it. Not what he's put in, but what he's left out!

TROUP. Oh this is the sheerest — the sheerest — how could he cover every contingency — look, you tell us that Stanley always gets at you through his orders — well, surely you examined him on every sentence when he took you through them.

BARTTELOT. I did not.

TROUP. Why not?

BARTTELOT. Perhaps, Mr Troup, because he didn't take me through them.

TROUP. That's irregular, I admit — but then he's not a military man — but you could have gone to him yourself, I suppose you read them before he left?

BARTTELOT. You suppose incorrectly. Mr Stanley made it impossible — quite impossible — for me to read them until he'd marched out of the Camp.

TROUP. But the fact remains there is nothing there to prevent you giving us our provisions. Good God, man, can you not see — I have two ounces of sugar, an ounce of tea — Mr Ward tells you he has nothing — Mr Bonny is out of —

BONNY. Tea.

TROUP. And the only reason you offer for denying us is that Stanley hasn't actually written it down that you should give us them. As if he didn't have enough on his mind —

BARTTELOT. Mr Stanley's last verbal orders to me, delivered before Jephson and Stairs as witnesses, was that I was on no account to exceed his written orders. On no account!

TROUP. You were on no account to exceed written orders that he prevented you from reading until he'd gone?

BARTTELOT. This is a trivial subject, trivial! There are more important matters — look outside, sir, at the state of the niggers Stanley's left us with — he made sure to take only the

healthy with him — don't doubt that — there's sickness,
pilfering — and you fret at me with your tea and sugar — by
God, I've said my last word on the subject. The subject is
closed! (*He exits through the flap*.)

TROUP. Well, it's not closed as far as I'm concerned — I've no
intention —

JAMESON. Mr Troup, your bed. Shall we go and find it?

TROUP. What? Yes, yes, the bed! At least I have a bed! (*He
laughs bitterly*.) I'm much obliged to you, Mr Jameson.
(*He follows* JAMESON *through the flap*.)

WARD. I remember a governess rather similar to the Major.
Her most infuriating prohibitions always depended upon some
illogically spiteful but unuttered edict of my father's. It's no
good blaming me, it's your papa says no. But he hasn't said
no. But he would if you asked him. In fact our papa hadn't the
slightest interest in us, and would have said yes to anything.
Did you have a governess like that, Bonny?

BONNY. No. But this governess'll say yes, don't you worry.

WARD. What makes you think that?

BONNY. Mr Jameson's face.

WARD. Ah, I see. That's why you kept the peace, was it?
Because you'd read Mr Jameson's face?

BONNY. Well, there was no good going on at him, was there,
it just made him more determined.

WARD. And did you like him for that?

BONNY. I didn't like him or dislike him. I recognised him for what
he is.

WARD. And what's that?

BONNY. Our Commanding Officer. (*He exits.*)

WARD *stares after him, then walks around the store-room,
stops to look at the turtles, then walks casually on to
Jameson's desk, picks up a sketch, studies it.*

JAMESON *enters, as if expecting to find the room empty.
Stops on seeing* WARD.

WARD. You've bedded old Troup, then?

JAMESON. He couldn't get off with it fast enough. He was
probably afraid I'd change my mind and wrestle it back
from him.

WARD. I was just admiring your work — it is yours, I take it?

JAMESON. Yes. A plover, he rested ten minutes on a branch right outside my tent this morning. I shall have to wait until I get home to do full justice to his colouring — the forehead's light brown — reddish brown, really — and the crest here (*coming over, pointing*) is blacker than I've managed with charcoal — so is the top of the head. And the cheeks are a delicate grey, as is the lower half of the throat. The whiteness of the paper is about right for the whiteness of the rest of the throat, but the wing crests are a wonderful ash-green — and no paper would serve for the white bar across the centre of the wing — and the eye — imagine an ochre iris around the black pupil.

WARD. That collection in one of the small huts — it's entirely yours then?

JAMESON. Why yes. Yes it is.

WARD. Good God, I thought it had been done by four men at least. A lepidopterist, an ornithologist, an entymologist and an ethnologist. What unified them must be the artist.

JAMESON. Or perhaps a dilettante, who separates them. Do you sketch, Mr Ward?

WARD. A little. Which is how I do most things. So I'm the dillettante, Mr Jameson, and now you've come face to face with the real article, you'll have to drop your pose. Unless, of course, it's assumed for the Major's sake.

JAMESON. Major Barttelot and I have been together in rather difficult circumstances recently. We've had to depend on each other too much, in sickness, and in health, to assume poses with each other.

WARD. Good Heavens, that sounds rather like a marriage!

JAMESON. I already have a marriage.

WARD. Really? And children?

JAMESON (*after a pause*). Two. At least I trust and pray two. The second was due last month.

WARD. May I congratulate you. Not least on your wife, who must be very understanding.

JAMESON. She is, Mr Ward. Thank you.

WARD. Did Mr Stanley choose you to stay behind with the Major, or did the Major choose you, or did you choose yourself?

JAMESON. It was understood that Stairs was to be left behind, but at the last moment Mr Stanley changed his mind, and appointed me. Mr Stanley being Mr Stanley, he offered no explanation. Have you any further questions?

WARD. I'm sorry, I've been impertinent. It's just that — look — I know from my own experience of this continent how quickly one can come to brood on a subject when cut off — isn't it possible that you and the Major —

JAMESON. Went a trifle mad together? Yes, quite possible. Nevertheless Stanley did threaten to destroy the Major's reputation.

WARD. Why?

JAMESON. Perhaps the Major wasn't used to being spoken to as Mr Stanley is used to speaking to gentlemen who accompany him on his expeditions. And Mr Stanley was even less used to being answered as the Major answered him.

WARD. And because of this — this clash of temperaments, Stanley would go to the length of ruining a man —

JAMESON. At the moment, Stanley is almost as powerful in London as he is in Africa. He'd only have to speak a few words — and Stanley is too jealous of his own fame to care much about another man's honour. The Major is a military man from a military family. His honour means a great deal to him.

WARD. Yet Stanley did make him Commanding Officer of his Rear Column. That could be construed as an honour.

JAMESON. It could also be construed as one of his insults. The Major was appointed Senior Officer to the Relief of Emin Pasha, and has been left behind to guard the supplies. He is a brave and active man, rendered temporarily inactive.

WARD. A sort of Samson, blinded and chained. And yet you were left with him — so Stanley showed some compassion to the Major. And to the rest of us, I suspect. Bonny has already singled you out as the peacemaker.

JAMESON. We had all of us better keep the peace, Mr Ward.

WARD. Oh, I shan't give you any more trouble, my word on it. And old Troup is really a decent enough fellow who's never been to the Congo before and has been out of bed too long — one good night'll probably settle him.

JAMESON (laughs). Well, you've only to settle Mr Bonny, and we shall be all right.

WARD. Mr Bonny has already informed me that he's quite settled. It seems that he likes his Commanding Officers to be commanding, which the Major evidently is. Did you know, by the way, that he's the only white man on the whole expedition who's being paid for his services. Can that be because he's the only one among us whose services are worth hiring? Whatever you say about Stanley, his recruitment drive in London was a spectacular success — why, they said at the Falls he'd actually got some rich nincompoop to pay for the privilege of marching with him, God knows how much! (*He laughs.*)

JAMESON. One thousand pounds, Mr Ward, and in view of what I've learnt so far, I count it a bargain as well as a privilege. So the Major is for honour, and Troup, I presume, is for honour, and Bonny for money, and I for study — what about you, Mr Ward, what are you here for?

WARD. I'm a patriotic Englishman, Mr Jameson.

JAMESON. I see.

WARD. And as Emin Pasha is an eccentric German employed by the Egyptians to maintain their interest in South Equatorial Africa, it is surely the duty of all patriotic Englishmen to sign up with a Welsh adoptive American to rescue him from a rampaging Muslim. While at the same time helping the Welsh adoptive American to extend a little more Belgian influence along the Arruwimi River. Isn't it?

JAMESON. You believe the rumours then? That Stanley is really doing all this for Leopold of Brussels?

WARD. Certainly not. He's using Leopold of Brussels so that he can do it all for Stanley.

JAMESON. But if you don't believe the cause is noble —

WARD. Noble! (*He laughs.*) There are no noble causes in the Congo, and never have been. In the Congo there are only cannibals and other natives, Arab slavers, European interests and magnificent opportunists. Along with birds, butterflies and snakes, of course, for artists and naturalists like yourself.

JAMESON. Then what are you doing here?

WARD. I haven't the slightest idea. All I know is that after three years travelling around the continent, I was suddenly desperate for the sight of England. Nothing could have persuaded me to stay on another month except, it seems, the very first opportunity to do so. Stanley's expedition was the first opportunity. Perhaps it's simply the fickleness of the dilettante who decides to put up with something he's tired of, for a change, eh?

JAMESON. Or the impulse of a serious man who's not yet discovered what it is he came here to find out.

WARD. Unless, finally, I'm an unwitting agent of one of history's more grandiose schemes.

JAMESON. What would that be?

WARD. Why, to ruin the reputation of a certain Major — from Norfolk, is it?

JAMESON. Sussex, it is.

WARD. In his Sussex family, with his Sussex hunt, and in his London clubs. Think, if only Gordon hadn't fallen at Khartoum the Mahdi wouldn't be driving on to destroy Emin Pasha, Stanley wouldn't be in the Congo, and ergo: I wouldn't be quarrelling with the Sussex Major for my flour, coffee, sugar, tea and gentleman's relish, at Yambuya, on the banks of the Arruwimi River, in June, this year of Grace, 1887.

JAMESON (*laughs*). Well, whatever the whirligigs of history or fate, Mr Ward, I believe I'm glad they've brought you to us.

BARTTELOT (*enters through the flap*). Ah, you're still here then. (*To* JAMESON.) I was looking for Bonny, as a matter of fact. Thought I'd better find out whether he brought up any quinine. He's not in his tent.

JAMESON. Well, he hasn't come in. He went off some time ago.

BARTTELOT. Oh.

JAMESON. He may be having a shower.

BARTTELOT. Looked there. No one in the shower.

Pause.

WARD. In that case, I'll be able to have one. (*He goes towards the flap.*)

BARTTELOT. Don't forget, Mr Ward. Roast goat. Roast goat and palm wine at sun-down, eh?

WARD *exits.*

BARTTELOT. You've been having a chat with him, then?

JAMESON. Yes.

BARTTELOT. Ah. And what's he like — when he's not drawling out his sarcasms.

JAMESON. Oh, rather sympathetic. Certainly intelligent.

BARTTELOT. You like him, then?

JAMESON. I found him rather a relief. (*Hurriedly.*) I mean, from what I'd feared earlier.

BARTTELOT. God Jamie, I wish I had your knack — but by God, what a business, eh! Hardly arrived and they're set against me. Even Stanley couldn't have hoped for such a swift success — grown men at each other's throats — over what! Fortnum and Mason's! That's the joke of it! And that Troup — (*pacing about*) dead set, dead set against me —

JAMESON. Ward assures me that now he's got a bed he'll calm down.

BARTTELOT. What, a bed, how?

JAMESON. I remembered Parke's — the one for Jephson —

BARTTELOT. There you are, you see! And I didn't think of it — not at all, all I could think was that he was after me for one of Stanley's beds — and now the bad feeling's there!

JAMESON. We'll find a way to win them around.

BARTTELOT. Hah! You'd find a way all right, Jamie. (*Pause.*) If I weren't here.

JAMESON. Oh now come, old man, you mustn't give in —

BONNY *enters through the flap.*

BARTTELOT. Ah, Bonny! Here you are — I've been looking for you.

BONNY. One of the nigger boys only just told me, sir. I was talking to Troup in his tent.

BARTTELOT. What? Talking to Troup?

BONNY. Yes, sir.

BARTTELOT. Well Bonny, we'd better have a think about our medical supplies, eh?

JAMESON. I'll see you at mess. (*He exits.*)

BARTTELOT. Right, Jamie, at mess. Yes, first thing is to make sure we keep our supplies separate from Stanley's — Oh, that reminds me — here's a (*takes a little package from his pocket*)

as you're desperate, not much I'm afraid, almost at the end
myself, but enough to make you a pot at least.

BONNY. That's — that's very kind of you, sir.

BARTTELOT. Not at all. Not at all. (*Pause.*) Now there's one
other matter. I need your advice on. I've been ill.

BONNY. Yes. Mr Jameson mentioned that you and he —

BARTTELOT. This is something different. Something a medic
can't detect — (*Pause.*) I don't sleep at nights, not for months,
not since Stanley left, get the shakes, the fever, nightmares,
that sort of thing and I can't — I find my temper, well,
scarcely seems to be mine any more as if — how to explain it
— as if I were being — being poisoned, do you see?

BONNY. Well, you probably are, Major, from what Mr
Jameson was telling me of your diet here.

BARTTELOT. No it's not the diet, Jameson sleeps like a top
most nights. He has the same diet. These nightmares, I tell
you — and headaches — I can't go on with them. (*Pause.*)
Well? What do you — ?

BONNY. Morphine, sir.

BARTTELOT. Morphine! Certainly not. Morphine's not the
answer. (*He looks at him.*)

BONNY. No, Major, it isn't. The answer is obvious enough. A
return to a different life, different food, a different country. In
other words, the answer for you is England.

BARTTELOT *looks at him, waits.*

But as the answer's out of the question —

BARTTELOT. Why?

BONNY. I beg your pardon, sir?

BARTTELOT Why is it out of the question?

BONNY. Well — because you're in command here, sir.

BARTTELOT. It might be better for everybody if I weren't.
(*Pause.*) Jameson — is more — more fit.

BONNY. Mr Jameson isn't an army man, though, is he, sir?
He's a gentleman of leisure, from what I can make out.

BARTTELOT. Mr Jameson happens to be the finest man I've
ever met.

BONNY. But Mr Stanley appointed you the Commanding Officer.

BARTTELOT. But between you, you and Troup and Ward and Mr Jameson — you could — (*pause*) do you understand what I'm asking?

BONNY. Yes, I do.

BARTTELOT. Well then, man!

BONNY. I'm not sure my recommendation would carry much weight.

BARTTELOT. But you would write one for me?

BONNY. Naturally, sir. If you ordered me to.

BARTTELOT. Ordered you to?

BONNY. I could hardly write a letter recommending that you be invalided home, without your asking me to, first. Which you have done. And I agree.

BARTTELOT. With the recommendation?

BONNY. To write the letter. It is an order, isn't it?

BARTTELOT. Of course it isn't an order! What value would a letter have that I'd ordered you to write — good God man, you have qualifications, you can judge a situation and act accordingly. Nobody would challenge a doctor's findings.

BONNY. That's true, sir, yes. But then I'm not a doctor.

BARTTELOT. Not a doctor?

BONNY. I'm a medical orderly. And that's less than third class in the medical profession. Did you take me for a doctor?

BARTTELOT. I didn't think about it one way or another. I assumed you had medical experience, I assumed — as they signed you up — you'd be, yes, properly qualified —

BONNY. I'm properly qualified as a medical orderly. And a medical orderly's services come considerably cheaper than a properly qualified doctor's. I expect Mr Stanley took that into account when he appointed me.

BARTTELOT. In that case, we've been at cross-purposes, haven't we?

BONNY. No, sir. (*Little pause.*) Well, at least I understood.

BARTTELOT. What? What did you understand? (*He moves towards him threateningly.*)

BONNY. Well, that you wanted my assurance, in as much as I could give it, that you're fit to carry on.

BARTTELOT. You want me to stay, do you?

BONNY. Yes, I do.

BARTTELOT. Why?

BONNY. Because you're the Commanding Officer. And if we're to be here a while yet, then Mr Stanley will be getting further and further away from us. The country is dangerous, there are cannibals around, there could be fighting. And this Tippu-Tib, who sounds as likely to attack us as give us our nigger porters. We'd need you then, very badly, however nicely Mr Jameson were to run things in the meanwhile.

BARTTELOT. You'll do for me, Bonny. You'll do for me very well.

BONNY. Thank you, Major. (*Little pause.*) You'll do for me too, if I may say so. (*He turns, makes to go out, stops.*) Oh sir, I shan't —

BARTTELOT. What?

BONNY. Needless to say, it shall never be mentioned by me that this conversation took place. The others might misconstrue —

BARTTELOT *stares at him.*

BONNY. And thank you again for the tea, sir. Much appreciated. (*He goes out.*)

BARTTELOT (*stands, for a moment, then lets out an exclamation, loud, of despair. He begins to stride up and down*). Damn — damn — damned insolence!

He drives the point of his stick into the ground, plucks it out, strides up and down.

(*Bellowing.*) John Henry! John Henry! (*He continues to stride, and as lights fade to black, still striding and jabbing his stick into the ground, at the very top of his lungs.*) John Henry!

Scene Two

About an hour later. The stage is in darkness. JAMESON *enters.
through the flap. He strikes a match, puts it to the lamp.*
    BARTTELOT *is sitting at the table, his hands to his face.*
    JOHN HENRY *is sitting at the end of the table staring
straight ahead.*
    JAMESON *takes in the scene, quickly lights the other two
lamps, goes over to* BARTTELOT, *puts a hand on his shoulder.*

BARTTELOT (*jumps, removes his hands*). Oh – oh Jamie – there
    you are! Well, supper, eh? Manioc soup, prime cuts of manioc,
    pudding of manioc –

JAMESON. Not tonight, old man. Can't you smell the goat?

BARTTELOT. What, by God, yes – goat, eh, how did you –
    oh, oh yes, those others, they've arrived, it's for them. (*He
    looks, sees* JOHN HENRY.) What? (*Stares at him.*) Ah, that's
    right, there's a good boy, John Henry, told him to sit down,
    not on the floor like a monkey, but at the table, like a human
    being, eh John Henry – and then when I – I – you just sat on,
    eh? Yes, that's a good lad, now go and get the palm wine,
    John Henry. Palm wine. Fancy that. (*He gets up.*) Falling
    asleep – and a nice sleep, a dream not a nightmare, I've got a
    feeling the old pater was in it, we were walking across the
    paddocks, a spring morning – smelt something good – perhaps
    it was the goat, eh? Well, now I'm back, they'll be here in a
    minute –

JAMESON. Look, something's occurred to me that may help –
    What do you say to giving them half their six months'
    provision now, and leave it to Stanley to give them their other
    half when we get up with him. That way, you'll be recognizing
    their claim, while still respecting Stanley's ultimate authority.
    Do you see?

BARTTELOT. But it would still be a breach.

JAMESON. Yes, but if you don't give them anything then they
    could complain to Stanley and it might suit him to take their
    side. There was nothing in my orders, he could say, and no
    reason that you shouldn't have obliged these men.

BARTTELOT. And so he gets me either way! For being in breach
    of his orders if I do, or failing to exercise my command if I
    don't!

JAMESON. Ah, but if he says you shouldn't have given them even half their provisions, then Ward, Troup and Bonny would have to come to your defence, you see. And Stanley wouldn't like that.

BARTTELOT. I don't know, Jamie. I don't know. All I know is that I'm well and truly in Stanley's web and whatever I do — I'll have to think — make a decision — but you believe that would be all right, do you?

There is a pause.

Look, old man, I must tell you. I — the fact is, I've just done something rather shameful. I asked Bonny if he could have me invalided home. (*He looks at* JAMESON, *distressed.*) It suddenly seemed a solution, you see, that as a medical man he could get me out of all this — a letter would do it, that was my thought. Then you and the others could do as you like, wouldn't have me to contend with. I'd be out of his trap honourably and the rest of you'd be out of his trap too, d'you see? But it's not to be. He's not a doctor, it turns out. Just a medical orderly. I'd have to order him to recommend me to leave — you can imagine what Stanley would have made of that — how he could get at me as far worse than a coward — a cunning coward. Eh? (*He laughs.*)

JAMESON. Poor old boy. I don't blame you, not at all, I'm only sorry —

BARTTELOT. No, don't be soft on me. I did wrong. I shouldn't have tried. But you know, there's something I want you to understand. I couldn't have done it. Couldn't have left, I'm sure of that. All I wanted was the letter in my pocket, that meant I could if I wanted to, you see? Something I could — could touch as — to confirm I'd made a choice — a choice not to go back even though I'd been let off. I'd never desert. Not desert you, old man, after the two months we've been through. I count you my closest — my closest —

TROUP *comes through the flap.*

Ah, Mr Troup — well, I hear you have a bed, thank God for that, eh?

JOHN HENRY *enters with a jug.*

And here's the palm wine — on the table — there's a boy — now the glasses —

WARD *enters.*

BARTTELOT. Ah, here you are then, Ward — showered and — and — and one for Mr Ward too, John Henry — now the jug — be careful not to spill, we've only about a quart of the stuff left, old Jameson bought it from the cannibals, so you see they have their uses, Troup, eh? (*He laughs*.) Not brandy, I know, but not as fierce as you'd expect from a cannibal brew —

As JOHN HENRY, *having filled* WARD's *and* TROUP's *and* JAMESON's *glass comes to fill his,* BONNY *enters.*

Ah, Bonny — Mr Bonny first, John Henry — that's right, there's a boy, and now mine — John Henry's quite a little find of mine, used to be one of Mr Stanley's boys, eh, John Henry? He was in the tent the morning Stanley was leaving — Stanley's tent — all the hullabaloo and John Henry crying, weren't you, John Henry, because Stanley had chosen to take one of his other boys instead, heartbroken because of it, eh, John Henry? And when Stanley marched out — by God, what a business he makes of it, struts yards ahead of his officers — poor old Jephson in a terrible state of indecision, whether to keep him company or maintain a respectful ten yards behind, Parke and Stairs trying to look unconcerned, at the back, but getting caught up in the Zanzibaris who wouldn't move fast enough for all the damned fuss, drums rolling, pipes blowing, and all the time Stanley not seeing the farce of it all, strutting along eyes focussed on posterity by way of the London *Times* and his publishers, old Jameson did a marvellous sketch, one of the Soudanese he left for us to bury managed to die just as Stanley passed him, old Jameson got him in the sketch, eyes rolling, what was it you called it, A Faithful Zanzibari says his Farewell to H. M. Stanley, Esq. H. M. standing for His Majesty, hah, hah, not Henry Morton by God, and above it Jameson's put, what was it, homage to a great man. (*He laughs*.) And there was little John Henry trailing behind, blubbering away, right out of the Camp, hoping right to the end His Majesty would pardon him and take him along after all, but I knew he wouldn't, knew he'd send him back and next morning — next morning I kept a look out for him, found him skulking with the Soudanese, and took him on. After a shower, of course. Now John Henry showers once a day, don't you, John Henry, and is my personal boy, sleeps outside my tent — tell them how Mr Stanley came by you, John Henry.

JOHN HENRY. Tippu-Tib, he give me Mr Stanley.

BARTTELOT. That's right, our old friend Tippu-Tib. He

captured John Henry from one of the villages, and made a
present of him to Stanley the last time Stanley was in these
parts. Stanley made him his chief boy, then when he went
back to England, stuck him in a missionary school at the Pool.
Collected him when he got back three months ago. And leaves
him behind all over again. Jameson and I've spent hours grilling
him about Tippu-Tib, haven't we, Jamie, but he only knows three
things about him, Tell us, John Henry, is Tippu-Tib a good man,
good man?

JOHN HENRY. Tippu-Tib good man.

BARTTELOT. And is Tippu-Tib a bad man.

JOHN HENRY. Bad man, bad man.

BARTTELOT. Now tell us why he's called Tippu-Tib? Why name
Tippu-Tib?

JOHN HENRY (*lifts his arm, points it about*). Tippu-tippu-tippu,
tib, tib, tippu tib, tippu tib.

JAMESON. Onomatopoeic, you see.

BONNY. What?

JAMESON. The noise of the rifle, when Tippu and his men come
firing on the villages. Far more exact than bang, really.

WARD. Tippu's real name is Hamed bin Mahamed el Marjebi. But
I never thought to ask why he was known as Tippu-Tib —

BARTTELOT. No, but Jameson did, eh Jamie? Anyway, those
are the three things that John Henry knows about Tippu-Tib,
that he's good, that he's bad, and how he got his name.

WARD. Which is one thing more than we know about most
people.

BARTTELOT (*laughs with false enthusiasm*). Very neat, Mr
Ward. Very neat.

JAMESON. Gentlemen, before you finish your glasses, may I
propose a toast. To the Rear Column.

BARTTELOT. To the Rear Column.

TROUP.)
WARD.) To the Rear Column!
BONNY.)

BARTTELOT (*catches Jameson's eye*). I've been thinking —
rather Jameson and I've been putting our heads together —
and what do you say to this? Three months provision now,

three months when we catch up with Stanley. Eh? What do you say? Troup?

TROUP. Well, sir, given your — your uneasiness with Mr Stanley's orders, that seems fair enough.

WARD. I think it's a marvellously sensible compromise. (*Glancing at* JAMESON.)

BONNY. Certainly do for me.

BARTTELOT. Very well, gentlemen. Now I've something to show you.

He looks to JAMESON, *winks, goes to a crate, brings it over, swings it up, jabs the point of his stick in, prises up the lid, and begins to plonk down items.*

One and a half pounds of coffee. One pound of tea. One and a half tins of salt. One and a half tins of jam and of chocolate milk. One tin of cocoa and milk. One tin of sardines. One of sausages. One pound of fancy biscuits. One third of a tin of red herring. Half a pound of flour. One pot of Liebig. One quarter of a pound of tapioca. Times three, of course.

During this drums have begun to pound.

TROUP. Oh, I see, This is a *month's* rations.

BARTTELOT. No, this is three months.

WARD. Three months' — that!

BARTTELOT. It is.

TROUP. But good God, who made up these provisions?

JAMESON. Fortnum and Mason's. They'd have done us quite nicely for an afternoon at Lord's Cricket Ground, don't you think?

TROUP. Good God, good God!

BARTTELOT. So there you, gentlemen! One half of what we were quarrelling about. And now perhaps you'll understand something about Mr Stanley, the greatest African explorer of our age! He has his expedition provisions made up by Fortnum and Mason's. (*He laughs.*)

The drums increase in volume.

Now if you excuse me while I put a stop to the accompaniment — (*He goes to the doors, unlatches them, throws them open.*)

From outside, fires flaming; low keening sounds; the drums louder; dim shapes everywhere. BARTTELOT *strides into their midst, with his stick.*

JAMESON. The Zanzibaris — the Major has a running battle with them every night —

BARTTELOT (*off*). That's enough of the drums — damn you, enough I say —

The drums diminish, without stopping.

JAMESON. There's a particular couple I call the Minchips because it's a Dickens-sounding name, and they're both out of Dickens — he'd have set them in the Mile End Road. The husband's as lazy a vagabond as you could expect to meet — lies on his side all day while the wife collects wood, bargains for food, gathers manioc — then at night after he's eaten he retires to his tent and cleans his rifle while the wife plays for him on the drums, I think she starts all the others off, and she's always the last to stop —

BARTTELOT (*still shouting, off*). Quiet I say — quiet —

WARD *goes towards the door, watches.*

TROUP *joins him.*

BONNY *pours himself some more palm-wine.*

There is now only one drum beating.

JAMESON *goes over to his desk, picks up the picture, looks at it.*

Drum plays a few seconds longer, then stops.

On this tableau:

Lights.

Curtain.

Act Two

Scene One

The Same. Six months later. Morning.
The doors are open. Outside, blazing sun-light and intense heat. Off, the sound of a voice, faint and unidentifiable, although it is Ward's. A thudding sound, also faint, follows each count.

WARD. Forty-five, forty-six, forty-seven, forty-eight, forty-nine, fifty, fifty-one, fifty-two, fifty-three, fifty-four, fifty-five, fifty — (*Stops, pause.*) Take him down, will you? Down! Take him down!

Movements, voices off. There is a pause.

TROUP enters through the main doors, goes to the water bucket, pours himself a mug of water, sits down, wipes his forehead, drinks.

BONNY enters. He is carrying salt and bandages. He puts them in a box. Goes to the water bucket, pours himself a mug of water.

BONNY. Jameson's due back this morning, isn't he?

TROUP. Is he? (*Pause, sips. Laughs.*)

BONNY (*looks at him*). What?

TROUP. Well, you're not setting any store by that, are you?

BONNY. Not setting store by it, no. Just wanting to find out.

TROUP. Well, you don't have to wait for him — I can tell you. There're rumours. As he knew before he left.

BONNY. There're rumours in the villages here. They may turn out to be facts further down.

TROUP. They're always rumours, never facts.

BONNY. But he thought these were worth following up.

TROUP. Of course he did. As they coincided with a distasteful duty.

BONNY. Oh well, can't say I blame him. He's a gentleman, after all.

TROUP. And the rest of us aren't?

BONNY. Oh, I only meant he's not an officer.

TROUP. Some of us try to be both. Not that I blame him either, if he can get away with it. But I wonder that Barttelot lets him, he wouldn't let me, or Ward, it's a collective responsibility, we take votes on it, we should all stand by the decision.

BONNY. But Jameson voted against, didn't he? This time.

TROUP. This time, last time and the time before.

BONNY. Still, what would be the point of a vote, if we all had to vote one way.

TROUP. That's not my complaint.

BONNY. But what is your complaint?

TROUP. Only that Jameson doesn't take any of the —

BARTTELOT (*off*). Here you nigger — move that nigger out of the way —

BONNY. What?

TROUP. It doesn't matter.

BARTTELOT (*enters, followed by* JOHN HENRY). Water.

JOHN HENRY *goes to the cask, pours a mug of water.*

BARTTELOT. Ward went over. Over by five. We entered fifty on the log, damn nuisance!

JOHN HENRY *brings the mug over to* BARTTELOT, *who swills it down, hands the mug to* JOHN HENRY, *who goes over, pours more.*

BARTTELOT. Jameson should be back by now, he likes to get in before the heat — God what a business, Ward going on, thought he'd never stop. (*He takes the mug from* JOHN HENRY *again, drinks.*)

BONNY. No, but I don't understand what your complaint is.

TROUP. It doesn't matter.

BARTTELOT. What complaint?

There is a pause.

BONNY. About Mr Jameson's absence, wasn't it?

BARTTELOT. What about his absence?

TROUP. I was just saying that it was unfortunate that Jameson missed the flogging.

BARTTELOT. Why? Do you think he would have enjoyed it?

TROUP. They're meant to be a joint responsibility. We're all supposed to stand by the majority decision.

BARTTELOT. And when has Jameson rejected the majority decision?

TROUP. My point is simply that he should see it through with the rest of us.

BARTTELOT. He's seen enough of them to know how they go.

TROUP. But he voted against, and then stayed away.

BARTTELOT. And so?

TROUP. It's a way of keeping in the clear, isn't it?

BARTTELOT. Clear of what?

TROUP. The responsibility, of course.

BARTTELOT. Oh, what are you talking about, Troup? Somebody had to go up river to check the rumours —

TROUP. And does that someone always have to be Jameson? And always when there's a flogging?

BARTTELOT. Jameson goes because he's learned the lingo and is good with the natives. All right. (*Pause.*) All right?

TROUP (*grunts*). He'll bring back some sketches.

BARTTELOT. What?

TROUP. I said he'll bring back some nice sketches, of birds and leaves and toads and butterflies, and whatnot, I expect.

BARTTELOT. Let's hope he brings back some news of Tippu-Tib, eh?

TROUP. Whether he does or not, he'll bring back some sketches.

BARTTELOT (*after a pause*). Well?

TROUP. Well, he's down in the log as dissenting, *and* down in the log as absent from proceedings. In the six months I've been here he's not supervised the floggings once.

BARTTELOT. And in the six months you've been here you haven't stopped complaining, to one of us about the rest of us, to the rest of us about one of us, if it's not the flogging it's wood patrol, if it's not wood patrol it's — it's something else.

BONNY. I'm sorry if I've given you cause for complaint.

TROUP. You still haven't answered the facts, have you?

BARTTELOT. What facts?

TROUP. I've done my turn on the floggings, Bonny's done his, you've done yours and so's Ward.

WARD (*entering wearily*). Done what?

TROUP. Your turn on the floggings.

WARD. Over-done it, I think, didn't I? This time.

BARTTELOT. By five strokes, what came over you, anyway?

WARD. Sorry. I didn't keep count of my counting. Let's just hope he didn't, either.

BONNY. He couldn't. Anyway not after the first twenty. He wasn't conscious.

WARD. How very fortunate. After all, what would one do if he asked for the last five strokes to be taken back. (*He laughs weakly.*) Anyway, I gave orders for two days remission in chains, hope that's all right?

BARTTELOT. What! No, it's not all right! You should have spoken to me first.

WARD. Yes, well, sorry again. I felt as it was my mistake I must make up in some way —

BARTTELOT. You made the mistake, it wasn't for you to make it up.

WARD. Well, what do you suggest we do? Eh? Eh? (*Fiercely.*) Anway, what difference does it make whether it's three or five, he won't last the night, will he Bonny?

BONNY. I shouldn't think so.

WARD. There! You see! (*Puts his face in his arms.*)

TROUP. You all right, old man?

WARD. Yes, yes, thank you.

TROUP (*to* BONNY). You'd better give him some quinine.

BONNY. Is that all right, Major?

BARTTELOT. How are the stocks?

BONNY. Beginning to run low.

TROUP. Still, if a man's ill, he must have medicine.

BARTTELOT. He can only have medicine if there's medicine to give him.

TROUP. But it's no good making sure there's medicine to give him by not giving him any.

WARD (*laughs*). Very neat, Troup, very neat.

TROUP. It wasn't meant to be. Because it's not funny when you think about it. If Barttelot starts refusing us medicine —

BARTTELOT. I've never refused when Bonny's said it's absolutely necessary. Nevertheless the fact remains there soon won't be any medicine.

WARD. Oh, don't squabble over my health, I'm all right, I tell you, short on sleep, that's all, my tent isn't conducive to it, the glow from their fires throws up peculiar images and their voices go on very shrill and the whole effect — you know it occurs to me, at least it did occur to me, when I'd counted to twenty-three strokes or twenty-four, somewhere in that passage anyway, the twenties it did occur to me that old Jameson was quite right, he usually is, you know, when he put forward the argument that we should abandon flogging for a while, we really are losing them fast enough at what's the current rate, one and an eighth a day Bonny worked it out at, from starvation, sickness etc, for us not to need to flog them to death too.

BARTTELOT. It's the one matter on which Jameson is not right. We have no choice. If a nigger thieves or deserts or trades his rifle for food or sleeps on sentry duty, he is to be flogged.

TROUP. But we do have a choice, that's what I was saying. If Jameson votes against, and now Ward votes against, it only needs one more vote — then what would you do?

BARTTELOT. I see. You intend to vote against, do you, in future.

TROUP. Or Bonny might.

BARTTELOT *turns, looks at* BONNY.

BONNY. What, me? Of course I wouldn't.

BARTTELOT (*to* TROUP). Well?

WARD. If Troup votes against, I shall have to vote for. I agree
with the Major. But I'll tell you what, Troup, shall we make a
deal, take it in turns, that way we honour the law and
satisfy conscience, how many judges manage that? With the
Major's permission of course.

BARTTELOT. I don't give a damn what you do between you as
long as discipline is maintained. If you all voted against I'd
enter it in the log and still have them flogged. And by God!
order whichever of you I wanted to supervise it. And now
that we've cleared that up, I've work to do — (*He exits.*)

WARD. Work, what work?

BONNY. He's counting the brass-rods. He started last night, in
here. I was just going to bed, he came bursting in, didn't even
notice me, started pulling the cases out — then at dawn he was
into the tents —

WARD. Well, it put him in a good humour for the flogging, didn't
it? I saw him joking with a couple of Zanzibaris just before I
began the count, you were at his side Bonny, as you usually are,
was it a good joke?

BONNY. It wasn't a joke. He was grinning at them.

WARD. Grinning at them?

BONNY. He's discovered that they're more frightened of him
when he grins at them.

WARD. Really? Well he's got an excellent set of teeth. Why,
that might solve our problem, instead of lashing a man to the
post and having him flogged, we can lash him to a post and
have Barttelot grin at him. Fifty, fifty-five times, it wouldn't
make any difference . . .

BONNY. Yes, it would. They'd go off from fright even quicker.

TROUP. They hate him.

WARD. They hate us all.

TROUP. But they hate him most. He goes out amongst them
looking for trouble, poking at them with his damned stick, as if
trying to stir them up.

BONNY. Perhaps that's what he's trying to do. Stir them up to
life. Hate might sustain them a day or two longer —

TROUP. That's not why he does it. He does it because he hates them back.

WARD. So do I.

TROUP. What?

WARD. When I see them lying about in the compound, in their sickness, as if they were the image of sickness itself. Or while they stand there, heads lolling, while I supervise one of them flogging another of them to death. That makes me hate them.

TROUP. We can't go on week after week — something must be done, and soon.

BONNY. But what do you propose, Troup?

TROUP. Simply that we do something, anything, to get on the move. Look here, Bonny, this is confidential.

WARD (*laughs*). Yes, do be discreet old man. By the way, that woman I saw you with last night —

BONNY. What? What woman?

WARD. I saw you in silhouette, tip-toeing past my tent —

BONNY. Then you were seeing things.

WARD. Yes, lots of things, you and the woman among them. But you've got a way with the ladies, haven't you? Old Troup here was telling me the other day how you managed coming out on the boat, you had to travel tourist as you were on the expedition's expense, isn't that right, old man, but before you were three days out — you did say three days, didn't you, Troup? You'd insinuated yourself among the ladies in First Class, by making free with little remedies for *mal de mer*, and ended up dining between two absolute beauties, Troup called them, didn't you, Troup, at the Captain's table. Two absolute beauties?

TROUP. Look here, Ward, I didn't mean — I didn't intend any slight —

WARD. Of course you didn't, he was most complimentary about your gifts, Bonny, he didn't end up at the Captain's table between two absolute beauties, did you, Troup, even though you went first at your own expense, he was envious, you see, so there's nothing to be ashamed of in taking a Zanzibari or Soudanese or native lady by the neck, eh, as long as there's no outraged husband —

BONNY (*gets up, comes over*). Lift your arms.

WARD. What?

BONNY. Lift your arms.

WARD *does so.*

BONNY (*feels in Ward's arm-pits*). Swollen. (*He puts his hand to Ward's brow*). You'd do better lying down.

WARD. No, I wouldn't.

BONNY. Well, if you don't lie down soon, you'll fall down later.

WARD. Right. I'll wait until then.

BONNY. Then you're a fool. And that wasn't me or a woman you saw last night, it was your delirium.

TROUP. Look here, let's get back to what's important. Can I speak plainly?

WARD (*laughs*). Plainly, Troup. Good God! You certainly can.

TROUP. What, look, I'm not advocating going behind Barttelot's back, but simply that we all have a reasoned and proper discussion –

WARD (*gets to his feet, as sudden noises off*). He's here!

TROUP. What?

JAMESON *enters through the flap. He is carrying a shoulder-bag.*

WARD. Welcome back, old man. (*He shakes his hand.*)

JAMESON. Thank you. Troup – Bonny – how are you –

TROUP. Any news?

JAMESON. Oh, nothing very definite, I'm afraid, although –

BARTTELOT (*comes striding in*). Ah, here you are then, Jamie, thank God, I was getting worried, well, what news, what news?

JAMESON. None really, I'm afraid. Lots of rumours, but I didn't actually find a native who'd seen an Arab. Mark you, there was a great deal of excitement, more than usual, but the only significant thing was that in the village by the second river bend – where the Chief wears those boots Stanley gave him – a more preposterous figure – (*He laughs.*)

BARTTELOT. Well, what about him?

JAMESON. I know it doesn't sound much, but you see, he claimed he hadn't heard anything at all, not even a rumour.

TROUP. It certainly doesn't sound much, other than that there might be one honest nigger in the Congo after all.

JAMESON. No, my impression was the opposite. I couldn't be sure the other chiefs were telling the truth, but I was quite sure he wasn't. He knew something —

BARTTELOT. By God, you mean you believe he's seen Tippu-Tib?

JAMESON. Not quite that. But perhaps an Arab or two.

BARTTELOT. But by God, that's something. That's something more than we've had this last six months!

TROUP. But you're only guessing. It doesn't seem much to me, to go on.

JAMESON. There was one small piece of evidence. Just outside his village I came across the remains of a feast, a few bones —

BARTTELOT. An Arab feast?

JAMESON. Oh no, quite distinctly a native feast. But an exceptional one. An Arab might have furnished it.

TROUP. Furnished what? A goat?

JAMESON. No, no. Himself. He might have been caught and eaten. But really there was no way of knowing, because if it was an Arab, he was presumably in the belly of the Chief who said there wasn't.

WARD. That's what's called digesting the evidence.

JAMESON. There were only a few digitals sucked clean and a couple of shin bones to go on. It could equally well have been a nigger from one of the other villages who'd come up too far, and the chief might well have been emphatic about there being no Arabs because he didn't want a fuss over his meal. I can't say.

BARTTELOT. And nothing else?

JAMESON. No.

BARTTELOT (*after a pause*). So we're no further ahead?

JAMESON. Not really. I'm sorry.

BARTTELOT. Not your fault, old man.

JAMESON. Still, the bearer of no news — I say, (*to* WARD) you don't look at all well, your fever still running?

WARD (*gestures*). Oh, I'm much better. Much.

JAMESON. That's good. By the way, I caught the most beautiful parakeet, I shall have to stuff him this evening — and look — (*He takes a sketch out, shows it to* WARD.)

BARTTELOT (*to* BONNY). You'd better come and have a look at a Soudanese lying on the bank, some sort of green bile coming out of his mouth —

WARD. Ah, and here's our Stanley-booted Chief. Yes, I see what you mean, embarrassed but replete — certainly a large, illicit meal not far from his memory —

TROUP. No! no! (*Suddenly loud.*) What are we going to do? Are we going to look at Jameson's sketches, or study sick Soudanese we can't do anything for anyway, or are we going to talk, to talk for once about what we're going to do? This situation can't go on, don't you see, Barttelot, you Jameson, surely you see — all we have to show for six months' waiting, for some sixty dead men, is a loathsome story of shin bones and cannibalism. It's the last straw. (*Pause.*) Don't you see! We must act! We must act!

BARTTELOT. And what action do you suggest we take?

TROUP. Stanley can't possibly want us to linger on here —

BARTTELOT. I assure you he does.

TROUP. Well, for how long? Another month? Another two months? What use will we be to him then? He might already have reached Emin Pasha, for all we know. He might even be dead, they might all of them have been massacred by the Mahdi —

BARTTELOT. Yes.

TROUP. And meanwhile we're to go on waiting?

BARTTELOT. Yes.

TROUP. Rot among rotting niggers for no reason? Or wait for them to turn on us when we're in the middle of one of our floggings and tear us to pieces, do you really think that's what Stanley would want? Tippu-Tib's not coming. We all know it. There will be no six hundred porters. There's nothing to wait here for —

BARTTELOT. Except one's honour.

TROUP. Your honour, you mean, with Stanley. Oh, come man, your silly feud with Stanley is eight months past, he's long forgotten it, if he's even alive. Don't you see —

BARTTELOT. I see what you're proposing. It's desertion.

TROUP. I'm proposing that we act with common sense. I tell you, Barttelot, whatever you may claim, Stanley is not a murdering maniac.

BARTTELOT. I never said he was.

TROUP The other night you accused him of attempting to poison —

WARD. A figure of speech, old chap. A figure of —

TROUP. Well, his attitude to Stanley is poisoning us, that's the point. Good God man, those orders of his you're so frightened of contravening, they were written on the supposition that Tippu would be here months ago — Stanley didn't even deal with the contingency that's arisen, he never expected it.

BARTTELOT. You've forgotten the brass-rods.

TROUP. What? You mean we're running out of those, too? Then we'll certainly have a rebellion to deal with, the only thing the niggers look forward to is their brass-rods —

BARTTELOT. We're not running out. Stanley's left us enough to pay the men for another six months. Another six months, Troup.

There is a pause.

JAMESON (*suddenly laughs*). No, just a minute old man, you've forgotten that we also have to pay Tippu's men on the march. He'd take that into account.

BARTTELOT. I did. If Tippu's men had been paid from the day Stanley left, we'd still have enough for another six months. As Tippu's men haven't arrived we've enough for another year and a half. This from Mr Stanley, who knows the value of a brass-rod in the Congo as a — a Jew does of a sovereign in Kensington. So there you are, Troup, there's your evidence, Stanley acknowledges through the brass-rods that we might have to wait, and wait, and wait.

There is silence.

TROUP. Then what about the quinine, how do you explain that?

University of Winnipeg, 515 Portage Ave., Winnipeg, Manitoba, Canada R

WARD. Perhaps he got Fortnum and Mason's to package the quinine.

BONNY. In my experience of medical supplies, there are never enough of them. Specially quinine.

TROUP (*goes to sit down*). Oh this is all — all speculation. The fact of the matter is, we don't know what Stanley intended — if only you'd found some way of getting him to take you through those damned orders. I still don't understand how it is you didn't get the chance, did he refuse to let you read them before he left, what?

JAMESON. I really don't see the value of going back —

BARTTELOT. No, I'll tell you what happened, Troup. I wasn't going to give him the satisfaction. That's what happened.

TROUP. What satisfaction?

BARTTELOT. Of watching me read them. When I went to his tent to get them he wasn't even dressed, that's how much — how much — he was just getting into those damned ridiculous togs he puts on specially for his marches, I had to stand there, to stand there while he crammed himself into those knicker-bockers he wears for showing off his calves and then his Norfolk jacket, which he thinks turns him into an English gentleman, and his German officer's cap, which he thinks turns him into a — a — German officer, and all the time strutting about gobble-de-gooking John Henry here who was blubbering away, and gobble-de-gooking the Soudanese in Soudanese and Zanzibaris in Zanzibari or the other way around for all I knew, to let me see the niggers were more important than his own senior officer, and sending messages to Jephson and Parke and Stairs — and in the middle of it all he shoved the orders into my hands and went on gobble-de-gooking, and when he saw I'd just shoved them into my pocket, that I was just going to go on standing there watching him with a smile he was forced to come back to me, and by God how he hates that, standing eye to eye with another white man. Well, Major (*He does a poor imitation of a high voice with a nasal twang.*) not interested in your orders? I take it, I said, I take it they don't apply until you've left the camp, Mr Stanley. Besides there's really no need, sir, as they shall be carried out to the letter, whatever they are. But not beyond the letter . . . or to your own letter . . . something like that, because I turned on my heel, and walked over here, leaving him to get on with his circus — so Troup, now you know why it was impossible, and why I wasn't going to give him the satisfaction, I hope it's given you some, eh?

TROUP. I can't believe it! You mean he actually invited you, — I can't believe it!

WARD. If you'll excuse the observation, old chap, one of your small weaknesses is that you can't believe what you clearly know to be true, it's far too human to be anything else, surely. You can believe it, can't you? If you try?

TROUP. Do you really find all this *amusing*, Ward?

WARD. Well yes, it's odd, I admit, but I put it down to my temperature or temperament —

TROUP. Well, because you didn't want Stanley to have the satisfaction, what it comes to is this. We have no idea what to do next —

BARTTELOT. We wait.

TROUP. For death?

JAMESON. Oh, I don't really think it'll come to that —

BARTTELOT. In view of the brass-rods anything else would be desertion. And that's what Stanley hopes for.

WARD. Well, actually Major, the brass-rods have nothing to do with anything at all. The perfectly simple and reasonable explanation for them came to me while you were describing — with great vivacity may I say — your last meeting with Stanley and then I became so engrossed with the — sorry — sorry — the delightful interchanges between yourself and our good Troup that I forgot to mention — and then you've such an assertive manner, do you see?

BARTTELOT. What are you talking about?

WARD. What?

JAMESON. It's his fever — (*goes to him*) old man, do lie down.

BONNY. I warned him.

WARD. Nonsense, no old boy, I'm quite — if you don't mind — the brass-rods, yes, the reason Stanley left them behind, yes, well it's because they're damned heavy, you see. Took as many as he calculated he'd need, and left us to bring up the rest with the porters, which porters and what porters being an entirely different question, but what would be the use of them if they weren't to bring up the brass-rods among the other things, eh?

There is a pause.

JAMESON. He's perfectly right, of course.

TROUP. Of course! My dear old Ward — well — so there we are, the rods mean nothing. Surely you agree?

BARTTELOT. It's a — possible — explanation.

TROUP. Well now can we — can we discuss it in a different atmosphere, I've been partly to blame, I admit, we bring out the worst in each other at times, eh, Major?

BARTTELOT. We wait. That's what we must do. For Tippu-Tib, or for a message from Stanley, or for news that Stanley is dead. We wait.

TROUP. No. No, I'm not going to wait. I'm going home. Who's coming with me? Ward, Jameson — you must see this is madness — come with me —

JAMESON. Excuse me, may I? (*Gently, takes* BARTTELOT's *stick.*) Stanley appointed me to stay with the Major, my place has been with him from the beginning — (*Moving gently towards* TROUP.)

WARD. There's no doubt honour's involved somewhere, you know, Troup, even if one can't — can't quite —

BONNY. I'm staying too. If you're interested, that is.

TROUP. Honour, there's no honour —

JAMESON *springs forward, with stick upraised, as if to strike* TROUP, *knocks him out of the way, and brings it down again and again, violently.*
TROUP *has lurched back with a cry of terror.*

JAMESON (*fishes up a dead snake with the tip of the stick*). Probably the mate of that one I got a few days ago — or were you simply after a spot of shade and a drop of water, can't blame you for that. (*He loops it over the rafters.*) You all right?

TROUP. What? All right? Yes, yes — what does another snake or two matter in all this madness.

BARTTELOT. When will you be leaving, Mr Troup?

TROUP. I can't go on my own, you know that.

BARTTELOT. One of us would accompany you, with the soundest of the Soudanese. We won't let you end up in the belly of an Arruwimi, don't worry.

TROUP. That's not what I meant. I stand by the majority decision.

BARTTELOT. We've each decided for ourselves, what our duty is. If you think yours is to leave —

TROUP. I'm staying.

BARTTELOT. In that case, Mr Troup, perhaps you will allow me to get on with my duties. Mr Bonny, shall we go and look at the Soudanese — (*He goes towards the flap.*)

BARTTELOT (*turns, looks at* TROUP). But by God, Troup, by God I shall put it in the log! (*He goes out.*)

TROUP. The log? What does he mean? We had a discussion, I stand by the majority decision — does he mean I was proposing to desert, to abandon you and Stanley — he can't put that in the log! I shall — I shall write a letter to the Committee in London, to Mr William MacKinnon himself, stating my position. I shall get it on record that there was never any question — never — (*He goes out.*)

WARD. I wonder who he thinks is going to deliver his letter, or perhaps he'll ask for a majority decision to pop over with it himself to, what's the address, somewhere in Cutter's Lane, Holborn, isn't it? I say Jameson, that's a fine specimen you slaughtered there, much better than its wife or husband, was it? Are you going to add it to your collection or have you got one already, how you sense these things! The way you moved I thought — I thought you were going to strike down old Troup or even the rest of us, all of us, a single blow, while you were away I've taken up sculpting again, but fretfully, fretfully, tried to model Herman and King, but they would keep their heads in, because of Bonny's remarks about cooking them, you know, I was looking forward to showing you, but it's rotten work, rotten work I'm afraid, I (*swaying as he speaks, and collapses just as*):

JAMESON (*gets to him quickly, to support him*). My poor old fellow — here — let me — better get you to bed —

WARD. No, not to my tent. Not to my tent, if you please.

JAMESON. Well then, come — (*He helps* WARD *over to settee.*) There, lie down.

WARD. Sorry, sorry, Jameson — did you know I went on to fifty (*very brightly*) five and a fraction, didn't matter though, Bonny says he'll die anyway, it became a bit hypnotic, you see, telling off the strokes, and he got into a rhythm you know, his arm sweeping back and then forward, and then the scream, and then my voice, and his arm sweeping back and the screams stopped, and my voice, and his arm, and my voice —

JAMESON. It must have been quite horrible for you.

WARD. No, no, it was quite pleasant, (*fretfully*) quite pleasant, don't you see, could really have gone on and on, why don't you do it, Jameson, don't you enjoy it, Troup says Barttelot lets you off, is that true?

JAMESON. I supervised it once or twice, before you other chaps came up.

WARD. And didn't you find it pleasant?

JAMESON. No. But I didn't have a fever when I did it, perhaps that helps.

WARD (*sitting up, very brightly*). What about your wife and child, children you pray and trust, it must be awful for them having you away, when people count on you so much, if we need you here she must need you there, do you ever think about them, do you, Jameson, do you worry if they're all right?

JAMESON. Yes.

WARD. And I worry about you, you know, when you're away, so does Barttelot tramping about at top speed ordering floggings and kicking niggers and grinning, have you heard about his grinning? And worrying about you, he misses you, doesn't he?

JAMESON. You're really rather ill, you know. You must try and sleep.

WARD. No, but Jameson —

JAMESON. You must sleep. You must.

WARD. But you'll look in on me later, won't you?

JAMESON. Of course. (*He goes to the doors, makes to shut them.*)

WARD. Oh, don't shut them, if you please.

JAMESON. Oh, I think so. They'll light their fires, and the din —

WARD. Oh, I don't mind, truly I want the light please.

JAMESON (*hesitates*). All right, I'll leave them half and half — (*He half closes the doors, then turns, looks at WARD, goes out through the flap.*)

The stage dims slowly to night. WARD is tossing and turning on his bed, in a troubled and feverish sleep.
Suddenly a blaze off, and cries. The light of a large bonfire getting brighter and brighter. Voices chattering.
The drums begin, as at the end of Act One.
WARD lets out a cry. Sits upright. The drums continue.
WARD stares wildly about, then fixes his gaze on the snake which appears, in the changing light from the blaze, to be writhing.
WARD stares transfixed, then begins to babble, shaking his head and clasping himself tightly. He is shivering. He moans, lets out shrill cries.
TROUP enters, through the flap, carrying a lamp. He goes to WARD's bed.

WARD. The worm, the worm — (*Pointing.*)

TROUP. What worm? (*He turns.*) Good God! (*Laughs.*) It's only Jameson's snake — (*He goes to the rafter, pulls it down.*)

WARD. Be careful — be careful — Jameson will want it.

TROUP puts the snake on the table, then goes to the doors.

BARTTELOT (*off*). Stop it, damn you! Stop it, I say!

TROUP. There's old Barttelot on his rounds again, eh? Having a go at Mrs What-d'you call her, Minchip —

BARTTELOT (*off*). Damn you, will you stop it!

The drums begin to quiet, as at the end of the previous scene.

TROUP (*closes the doors, comes over*). I say, old boy, you've got it badly, eh?

WARD (*is sitting up, shaking hideously*). You mustn't go away again, you mustn't leave me again.

TROUP. No, no, of course not, old man, I'll sit by you. (*He gently pushes WARD back.*) There now, old man, that's better, isn't it? I'll be here, you'll be all right, eh?

JAMESON enters through the flap, also carrying a lamp and some blankets, comes over, looks down at WARD.

Not too good, eh?

JAMESON. No. (*He begins to put blankets over WARD, assisted by TROUP.*)

WARD. Jameson, Jameson — you there. (*Teeth chattering.*)

JAMESON. Yes. Right here.

WARD. You will stay, won't you?

JAMESON. Yes. Yes, I'll stay.

BONNY (*enters through flap*). Here we are, some quinine, compliments of the Major.

TROUP. Thank God for that.

BONNY (*goes to* WARD, *lifts his head*). Now get this down you — (*He administers it.*) There we are.

WARD. Thank you, Jameson.

BONNY. He's very bad. Very bad. If he'd lain down at the beginning — somebody'd better stay with him.

JAMESON. Yes, I'm going to.

BONNY. Then the rest of us better leave him in peace.

TROUP. Right. If you're sure —

JAMESON. Quite sure.

TROUP. Well then — (*He puts his hand on* WARD'*s shoulder.*) Good night, old man.

BONNY. Good night.

JAMESON. Good night.

TROUP *and* BONNY *go towards the flap.*

BARTTELOT. Ah, you're all here are you, how is he?

BONNY. At the crisis. Jameson's going to sit with him.

BARTTELOT. Ah. (*He comes over to the bed.*)

TROUP *and* BONNY *exit.*

BONNY. Good night, Major. (*As he goes.*)

There is a pause.

BARTTELOT. He's had the quinine then?

JAMESON. Yes.

BARTTELOT. Ah. Well, be careful, Jamie, don't want you going out on us, we can take turns.

JAMESON. No, I'll be all right.

BARTTELOT. Ah. (*Pause.*) Well — (*He puts his hand on* JAMESON'*s shoulder.*) Good night, old Jamie.

JAMESON. Good night.

> BARTTELOT *hesitates, turns, goes out through the flap.*

> *There is a silence.*

WARD. Jameson!

JAMESON. Yes.

WARD. Jameson, are you there?

JAMESON. Yes, I'm here.

> *There is a silence.* JAMESON *sees the snake, goes over, picks it up, then draws a chair to the bed, arranges the lamp so that the light falls on him. He takes a knife from his pocket, and begins to skin the snake.*

> *On this, lights.*

Scene Two

Some days later. Night.
> *A brazier is the first glow, followed by the other lights. WARD's make-shift bed has been disestablished.* JOHN HENRY *is moving around the table, clearing away the remnants of a meal.* BARTTELOT, BONNY *and* TROUP *are seated around the brazier.* BARTTELOT *is smoking a pipe. After a pause,* JAMESON *gets up, goes to the brazier, stokes it up.*
> *Off, a single drum starts, very low, almost a murmur.*

BARTTELOT. There she goes.

TROUP. I can't hear her. Oh yes. Still, they're very quiet tonight. Do you think they know? I mean, they might have felt something today. From us. The way we've behaved.

BONNY (*laughs*).

TROUP. Well, she's beating very soft, and the others haven't joined in. How do you explain that?

BONNY. Not by sentiment, anyway. The wonder is she can play at all, after what the Major did to her last night, eh Major?

BARTTELOT (*as if not listening*). Mmmmm?

TROUP. Why does she do it anyway, what do you think, Jameson?

JAMESON. What? Oh — (*coming from the brazier to sit down*) for the magic, I should think. As long as Mrs Minchip plays, the sickness will stay off Mr Minchip.

BONNY. Seems to work. They die around him, but every morning he's as fresh as black paint, except for a few patches of red and blue from the Major's stick or boot, eh Major?

JAMESON. Yes, well it's really very reasonable. Mr and Mrs Minchip are evidently genuinely attached to each other. Her continuing to play the drums for him in spite of the Major's attempts to stop her, only proves it to both of them. And so provides them both with a reason for living.

BONNY. There you are, Major, you're part of her magic too.

BARTTELOT. Mmmm? What do you mean?

BONNY. Well, you're helping to keep their marriage together and that always takes magic. Are you going to go out to them?

BARTTELOT. No, no. Not tonight. It would be wrong tonight.

TROUP. And they *are* very low. I tell you they feel something of what we're feeling. (*Pause.*) There! She's stopped altogether!

WARD *enters through the flap. He is carrying a large tray, on which is an object covered with a handkerchief. Under his arm, a bottle of brandy.*

BARTTELOT. Ah, there you are at last. What have you been up to?

WARD. Gentlemen, my apologies for the delay. There's a little something I gave myself to, in an idle kind of way, during my convalescence that I hesitate to present to public view (*putting the tray on the table*) but I hope that my main contribution (*holds up the brandy bottle*)

Laughs and cheers.

will help to render the other more tolerable. And his own to the evening has been so extreme that, however inadequately, he must be honoured. So gentlemen, Troup old man, if you would — (*hands him the brandy bottle*)

TROUP *pours into glasses.*

While I propose, thank you old man, a toast —

OTHERS (*standing*). A toast!

WARD. To our tender and succulent benefactor! (*He removes*

the hankerchief, to reveal the head of a goat, modelled in clay.)

Exclamations and applause.

WARD. To dear old Nanny!

OTHERS (*laughing*). Dear old Nanny!

JAMESON (*studying it*). But look here, old man, it's a real piece of work, something really done — the mouth is wonderful, quite wonderful — the sardonic grin, the twist there of the lips, the very essence of goatiness —

TROUP (*belches*). The substance being somewhere else.

WARD (*to* JAMESON). I'm not thoroughly shamed by it, I admit.

BONNY. The funny thing is, I shall miss him.

TROUP. That's charitable, Bonny, considering the devil never stopped trying to kick you.

BONNY. The devil's always trying to kick me, in some manifestation or another.

JAMESON. Now the brandy's arrived — (*taking a newspaper packet out of his pocket*) may I present my little — (*Holding it out. They take from it a cigar each, with little exclamations.*)

BARTTELOT (*pocketing his cigar*). I'll hang on to this a little longer, by God, it's good, Troup, damned good! Thank you for it.

BONNY. We all owe Troup thanks for it. He's sweetened the atmosphere around you.

BARTTELOT. What? (*He looks at* BONNY.) Oh. (*He laughs.*) Neat Bonny, very neat.

JAMESON (*who has been about to thrust the cigar newspaper into the brazier, checks himself*). Good Heavens, here's something — the personal column. If the gentleman who waited outside the Savoy on Friday of last week at the appointed hour should care to do so again this week, he will receive a full explanation, and an assurance of —

TROUP. Assurance of what?

JAMESON. It stops there.

BONNY. An assurance of nothing, then.

TROUP. Or of everything.

JAMESON (*looks at date*). Fourteen months ago. Well, let's trust the matter's been settled between them, whatever it was.

TROUP. Oh, it's obvious what it was. The writer is a lady and her message is addressed to a — well, gentleman.

JAMESON. Well, go on, old man. Give us the whole scene.

TROUP. Well, well it's a sacred tryst, what? They meet, let's see, they meet every Friday, for a few precious moments. They don't touch, scarcely speak, look into each other's eyes —

JAMESON. And what happened on that last Friday?

BARTTELOT. I'll tell you what, she has a fierce pater who locked her in, and the gentleman in question's an officer — penniless but true, they're planning something dashing — an elopement — eh?

BONNY. Mark my words, it's either money or — the other thing. If it's the other thing he didn't turn up because he's tired of waiting for it, if it's money she's not giving the other thing until she's got her hands on it.

JAMESON. How does that end?

BONNY. Oh, in the usual way. With an arrangement. The question is how *that* ends?

WARD. How does it usually end?

BONNY. Why, if it's bad, in the law courts. And if it's worse — in church.

BARTTELOT. Careful, Bonny, careful.

TROUP. Oh, I say, why is that worse?

BONNY. Because then it never ends.

JAMESON. Ah, but that song, Bonny — the one you were humming in the shower — I believe you're a sentimentalist at heart, like all cynics.

BARTTELOT. What song?

BONNY. Oh, just a song —

BARTTELOT. Sing it for us.

BONNY. What?

BARTTELOT. Sing it for us. (*Little pause.*) Come on, Bonny!

BONNY, *after a moment, stands, sings a Victorian love song, delicately and with feeling.*

TROUP (*rises, emotionally*). Gentlemen, to a young lady — a young lady in Highgate!

REST. A young lady in Highgate!

BARTTELOT. And a young lady in Sussex!

BONNY. To a young lady in Pimlico. Another in Maidenhead. A third in Greenwich!

BARTTELOT. No no, only allowed one, Bonny.

BONNY. Ah, then I choose — a young lady in Clapham!

REST (*laughing*). A young lady in Clapham!

WARD. To them, all plain and pretty, amiable and otherwise the true, the false, the young, the old — so long as they be ladies!

TROUP. You're worse than old Bonny — you've taken them all!

BONNY. No, he hasn't. Just one. Pretty, amiable, young and true on the way to the altar! Plain, false, old and otherwise from there to the grave!

BARTTELOT. You go too far, Bonny! Too far! Remember Mrs Jameson!

BONNY. Oh, I'm sorry, I didn't mean to give —

JAMESON. Oh good Heavens, I can easily refute our Bonny — by inviting you all to take dinner in my home this day a year hence. Mrs Jameson and I and our (*hesitates*) children will be grateful for the chance to prove that what begins in church can continue ever more happily, please God! Will you come, all of you? Mrs Jameson would be so pleased.

BARTTELOT (*solemnly*). Mrs Jameson!

REST. Mrs Jameson.

A respectful silence.

JAMESON. Or of course, *two* years hence, depending on circumstances known to us all —

Laughter.

WARD. And that's the real interpretation to put on the message in the Personal Column — it's not written by a lady at all, but by some desperate fellow trying to do business with Mr Tippu-Tib. Who is now outside the Savoy —

JAMESON. Or indeed inside it, with his six hundred porters turned waiters.

Laughter.

BARTTELOT. You know what my pater says, he says 'It's a funny old world.' And he's right. Here we all are, we've had our quarrels and our worries, God knows — old Troup and I are a pretty peppery couple of fellows from time to time, eh? But here we are — and somewhere out there, Stanley, please God, as Jamie said — and tonight — well tonight, my spirit's at peace with him. I'll never like him, I can't promise to like him but by God I can't help wishing him safety, and an evening of fellowship like this one. Eh?

REST. Hear, hear!

TROUP. And I'll wager he's wished us the same, eh? And look, I want to endorse everything the Major's said — whatever — whatever the hazards — we are — we remain

BONNY *is quietly pouring himself more brandy.*

united, I mean we've forged a bond — between us — that — that — speaking for myself I know will last to the end of my life. I shall look back on this Christmas together to the — to the end of my life.

There is a pause.

JAMESON. Amen to that.

BARTTELOT. Bonny, give us a carol, there's a chap. My heart yearns for one.

BONNY *begins to sing 'The Twelve Days of Christmas'.*

OTHERS *join in. Half-way through the drums begin, very low, scarcely noticeable.*

BARTTELOT *has put his hand on* JOHN HENRY's *shoulder.*

As they sing, lights and:

Curtain.

Act Three

Scene One

The same. Six months later. It is morning.
  The doors are open. Around the room are various pieces of sculpture, in clay, heads of natives, animals, etc; and some sketches, stuffed birds, stuffed snakes.
  A NATIVE WOMAN, naked, her arms tied behind her, a halter around her neck and attached to a rafter, is squatting on the floor, right.
  WARD is seated on a packing case, modelling her head in clay.
  BONNY enters, drifts over, watches WARD, then sits down at the table, close to the woman. There is a silence. He stares at the woman, suddenly smiles at her.
  The WOMAN smiles back.
  BONNY laughs.
  The WOMAN laughs back.
  BONNY laughs again.
  The WOMAN laughs again.

BONNY. Funny, they squat for hours without an expression until you laugh at them. And they always laugh back.

WARD. Yes, they have very pleasant dispositions. Unless of course she was laughing at you for laughing at her — who can say whether the man is playing with the cat or the cat with the man . . .

BONNY. More like cattle than cats. Although she might have a game or two in her . . . eh, my darling? (*He laughs.*)

  The WOMAN laughs.

WARD. Could you, do you think, hold back on your wooing a while — I'd prefer her to keep her head still. Besides, the days when you were the Lothario of Yambuya are over by some months, aren't they — ever since our Commanding Officer delivered his *en passant* homily on what he'd do, by God, to any white man he caught, by God! etc, etc.

BONNY *yawns, puts his feet on the table, his head back. Begins to hum.*

WARD (*glances at him with irritation*). Why don't you join our Commanding Officer, he'd be glad of your company, I'm sure.

BONNY. Where is he?

WARD. Having a word.

BONNY. Who with?

WARD. A couple of Soudanese who fell asleep on watch last night. The second provisions tent, I believe it was. Some of Stanley's medical supplies are in there, so he should be lathering up nicely, you'll catch him at his climax if you run.

BONNY (*after a slight pause*). Anything missing?

WARD. Mmmm?

BONNY. Anything missing?

WARD. Why don't you scamper over and see for yourself, there's a good man.

BONNY *gets up, goes over to the water bucket, tries to pour himself some. It is empty.*

BONNY. John Henry! John Henry!

WARD. Oh for – do stop shouting, Bonny! He won't come. At least, not for you.

BONNY. Well, he'd better, for his sake. If the Major finds out he's forgotten the water – John Henry!

WARD (*throws down the clay in disgust*). He's probably unconscious, you fool.

BONNY. What? (*Little pause.*) Oh.

WARD. Didn't you hear his screams?

BONNY. No.

WARD. Really not? About midnight, from his master's tent?

BONNY. No.

WARD. Nor his master's bellow, stick and boot?

BONNY. No.

WARD. How do you manage those slumbers of yours? You seem

to have found the secret that eludes everyone but the niggers on watch and the dying, of course.

BONNY. Perhaps I've given up worrying.

WARD. But what have you taken up to give up worrying? (*He looks at him.*) Eh, Bonny?

BONNY. The thing about you, Ward, is you can't let up, can you? You set out to make him worse, the way you went on at him in mess, counting off the niggers who'd died or escaped this last month —

WARD. I was merely trying to engage his attention, with a little mental arithmetic.

BONNY. Yes, well you left him in a proper state, then banging your hand up and down to the drums — that's probably why he went off and battered John Henry.

WARD. Ah, I see. And that's why you needn't concern yourself with his health. Don't types of your rank have to take the Hippocratic oath, Bonny?

BONNY (*after a pause*). Oh, shut up, Ward.

WARD. You feel no professional obligation, to minister to him, eh?

BONNY. What am I meant to do? He hasn't consulted me, has he?

WARD. And he won't. He's far too frightened.

BONNY. What of?

WARD. You.

BONNY. Oh very funny, Ward.

WARD. You can have my next year's ration of goat if he isn't.

BONNY. You honestly mean to tell me that Barttelot's frightened of *me* —

WARD. Barttelot? Good God, Bonny, you'd better not go about confusing our Commanding Major Barttelot with his battered little nigger of a serving boy. No, no, get it clear in your head, they're fearfully distinct, you know. The battered little nigger of a serving boy is the one who's frightened of you, even though he needs your skill and bandages. The Commanding Major Barttelot is the one you're frightened of, and with good reason, as he's quite clearly mad. And now you've got something to report to the Major, you'll hurry along, won't you, please, and report it?

BONNY. You want me to tell him that you say he's mad, do you?

WARD. Yes please.

BONNY. Why?

WARD. So that I can tell him what it is you've started taking to give up worrying. Then he'll have you flogged, I should think, and I'd quite enjoy that. Wouldn't you?

BONNY. I warn you, Ward, if you make any trouble for me with Barttelot, I'll make a damned sight more back.

TROUP *enters. He looks very ill, thin and yellow complexioned.*

BONNY. Oh hello, old man, how are you?

TROUP *pays no attention, goes on to the water bucket.*

BONNY. You really shouldn't be up you know.

WARD. There you are, old man, Bonny's just made out his favourite prescription. That should make you feel better.

TROUP *drops the cup, comes back to the table, sits down.*

BONNY. I'll get you some water — (*He rises.*)

TROUP. No, you won't.

TONNY. You're thirsty, aren't you?

TROUP. Yes, but you won't get any water. You'll go out for it, but you won't come back with it.

BONNY. What do you mean?

WARD. You know what he means. He means that you'll go out for it but you won't come back with it.

TROUP. Because you haven't asked him, have you?

BONNY. I haven't even seen him to speak to this morning.

TROUP. But you're not going to ask him, are you?

BONNY. Of course I am. I said I would. But I also said I didn't see the point because we all know what the answer's going to be.

TROUP. What about you, Ward, will you speak up for me?

WARD. Of course. But I won't do any good, old chap. Quite the reverse, I'm afraid.

TROUP. I see. So I'm to die then? Is that it? To die without making a fuss.

BONNY. Look, I don't think it's quite that bad —

TROUP. Oh yes it is. Oh yes it is. I'm weaker every time I come out of it. I shall die all right, I've known it for days now. I shall die. Die here in this place because a lunatic, a lunatic — (*He stops, trembling.*)

WARD. I say, old man, be careful. The faithful Bonny, you know, is at your side.

TROUP. I don't care. I'm past caring. You tell him I saw him, Bonny. He didn't know I was watching, but I saw him, from my tent flap. I saw the lunatic go out and —

BARTTELOT (*enters, carrying his stick and a basket*). Two rotting fish! Two rotting fish!

WARD. Three dying niggers, four flogging gentlemen —

BARTTELOT. What?

WARD. Oh nothing, just what promised to be an amusing anecdote of old Troup's you've interrupted, what were you saying about two rotting fish —

BARTTELOT. That's all her husband thinks she's worth, smirking outside as if he were redeeming from a pawn shop — (*going over to the woman, untying the rope from the rafter*) come on, get up, get up, he's bought you back with two rotting fish — go on, get along with you — and take these with you — (*He hooks basket around her neck*) tell him to choke on them himself — (*He grins at her, she cowers away from him*) go, get along with you — (*He propels her out through the door*) swears there isn't a goat to be had, stinks like a goat himself, a morning wasted catching her for two rotting fish — well, I got them to admit it at last, they'd been asleep all right, thank God they hadn't got into the boxes, none of them opened and they're not cunning enough to put the lids back on — by God if any of the medicine had been touched Stanley'd never have believed it was the niggers — not with a chance like that — Troup, you're closest to the tent, did you hear anything last night?

TROUP. I'm still ill, thank you for asking. Worse, as a matter of fact.

BARTTELOT. What?

WARD. Still ill, thank you for asking. Worse as a matter of fact.

BARTTELOT. I'm talking to Troup, Ward.

TROUP. I said I'm worse.

BARTTELOT. But you're up, aren't you?

TROUP. Oh yes. Yes, I'm up, Barttelot.

BARTTELOT. Slept through the night, did you?

TROUP. No, Barttelot. No sleep. None at all.

WARD. Loyal Bonny did, though, didn't you, Bonny? Slept like a top.

BARTTELOT. Well then, did you hear anything, see anything?

TROUP. Oh yes. I saw and heard quite a lot.

BARTTELOT. What?

WARD. He saw and heard —

BARTTELOT. From the provisions tent?

TROUP. No. Not from there.

BARTTELOT. Well, Ward, what about you?

WARD. Screams, oaths and blows from your tent. From the provisions tent, nothing. So I'm afraid I can't help you either, sir.

BARTTELOT (*goes over to the water*). Well, we've got to find out who's responsible, there's a clutch of Soudanese scum who're up to some mischief — (*Tries to pour water.*)

WARD. How remarkable.

BARTTELOT. What?

WARD (*after a little pause*). Why, that anyone in the compound, apart from your energetic self, of course, could be up to anything as taxing as mischief.

BARTTELOT. Well, you're damned well not are you, been idling in here all day — John Henry, John Henry! Where is the little —

BONNY. Haven't seen hide nor hair of him, Major.

WARD. From which we can conclude, sir, that he must still be out.

BARTTELOT. Out where?

WARD. Of his senses. And after the kind of night you had together, it's not to be wondered at, is it?

BARTTELOT. You drank the last drop of water, I suppose, Ward, but damn if you were going to get some more for the rest of us, eh?

WARD. Damn me, sir, if I was.

BONNY. I'll go, Major, I was just about to fetch some for Troup anyway — (*Getting up.*)

BARTTELOT. Thank you Bonny.

WARD. Before you go, Bonny, would you kindly ask the Major what you promised old Troup here you'd ask him.

BONNY. What?

WARD. Before you go, Bonny, would you kindly ask etc.

BONNY. It's only what I've already mentioned, Major. I explained that the situation being what it is —

BARTTELOT. You know the situation, Troup. You've known it for months. There isn't any.

TROUP. Yes, there is. There is!

BARTTELOT. But it's not ours, Troup. It's Stanley's. We've used up ours.

TROUP. So. So I'm to die —

BARTTELOT. You're not going to die.

TROUP. — because the rest of you used up our stock before I could get ill, is that what it comes to?

WARD. Yes, even you must find that a trifle bizarre, sir. That poor old Troup's superior robustness has had such an unhappy effect on his health. (*He laughs.*)

BARTTELOT. What?

WARD. Yes, even you must find that a trifle —

BARTTELOT. By God, Ward, how sick I am of your jokes.

WARD. Ah, but fortunately — for you — you don't need quinine to recover from them.

BARTTELOT. But I know how to stop you making them.

WARD. So do I, sir. Some humanity, or failing that, a dash of intelligence, in the running of this camp. Or did you mean bellow, boot and stick, as usual.

TROUP. You're just going to stand by, then, and see me die, are you, Barttelot? My death shall be on your head. I've written to MacKinnon, my letter to be conveyed to him with the rest of my effects, Ward, if you'll be so good.

WARD. Of course, my dear chap. Though I should point out that having over a hundred dead blacks on his head already —

BARTTELOT. That's right, Troup. You can die if you want to. I've long wanted you gone, you've never had anything to give to the Rear Column but bluster when you're well and snivelling now you're sick. It's not medicine you lack, Troup, but fortitude.

TROUP (*after a pause*). You refuse me, then.

BARTTELOT. Of course I refuse you.

TROUP. And that's your last word?

BARTTELOT. I hope so. Though knowing you —

TROUP. Very well. I give you warning, Barttelot. I shall help myself from Stanley's supplies.

BARTTELOT. What? (*Pause.*) What did you say?

TROUP. I shall help myself —

BARTTELOT. By God — by God, you already have, haven't you? It was you, wasn't it, in the provisions' tent last night! It was you! I'm going to open every load, every one, and if there's a drop of quinine missing, I'll — by God, Troup, I'll have you flogged for the thieving nigger you are.

TROUP (*runs over to him*). You're mad, Barttelot, a lunatic, a lunatic! I saw you last night, I watched you, I wrote it down, It's in my letter to MacKinnon, don't forget the letter, Ward —

WARD. Certainly not, old man.

TROUP. Everybody'll know you for what you are — do you know what he did last night?

BARTTELOT (*advances on* TROUP, *grinning*). Hah, hah, hah, hah! Hah hah hah hah!

JAMESON *appears at the door. He is carrying equipment, as in Act Two, Scene One. He is not, at first, noticed.*

Hah hah hah hah!

TROUP. You, you —

WARD. Ah, welcome home, old man — oh, the Major and Troup are just sharing a joke on the subject of the Major's sanity.

BARTTELOT. Hah hah hah hah!

TROUP *draws back a fist, to strike* BARTTELOT. BARTTELOT *thrusts his face closer to* TROUP.

Hah hah hah hah!

JAMESON *moves very swiftly, catches* TROUP's *arm, pulls him away. He stands between* BARTTELOT *and* TROUP, *facing* BARTTELOT.

Ah — ah, there you are, Jamie, you're back then are you?

TROUP. He's trying to murder me, murder me, Jameson — well — (*trying to pull* JAMESON *away*) let him do it so everybody can see — go on, Barttelot, kill me, kill me now, in front of everybody —

BARTTELOT. By God I will, Troup, if you don't get out of the Camp and back to England. I'm sending you home, now, this minute.

TROUP. See, see, he's frightened of me because I saw him — Oh, I saw him —

JAMESON. Please. Please, listen to me. (*Little pause.*) I've news. I've seen Tippu-Tib.

BARTTELOT. What? (*As if dazed.*) Seen him?

JAMESON. Yes. He sends his greetings and his apologies for the delay.

BARTTELOT. The delay! For the delay — after a year!

JAMESON. But he solemnly undertakes to be with us shortly, with the porters. He swore it to Allah, and in friendship to Stanley. Apparently he lost his first catch through a series of monstrous misfortunes — escape, sickness, capsizing boats, but he sent messengers to let us know — presumably they were the cannibal victims. But his second lot, with a large guard of his Arabs, are on their way. He's just had word. He's going back to the Falls to bring them up himself.

BARTTELOT. About — about three weeks then! A month at the most!

JAMESON. His own calculation was a month.

BARTTELOT. By God — by God — of all the wonderful — but what was he doing in these parts, if his slaves are at the Falls?

JAMESON. Coming to see you. But I told him that as he'd seen me, you'd prefer him to get back to the porters —

BARTTELOT. By God yes — and Stanley — any news of Stanley?

JAMESON. He must be alive as he'd have heard if he were dead.

He's a rather extraordinary chap, our Tippu, by the way, you'll enjoy —

BARTTELOT (*is pacing about, talking almost as if to himself*). So Stanley's still alive, the porters coming up — can't be more than a month away — we'll meet him on the march, by God — with the loads — with the loads — how d'you do, Mr Stanley, here are your supplies, sir — by God we've beaten you, Stanley — beaten you, sir — (*He goes on out through the doors, and his voice, off.*) Up on your feet, scum, up on your feet, you're going to learn how to walk again — up I say — up with you — by God I've beaten him — march — march along I say — I've beaten the devil — (*His voice fading, but sounding now and then.*)

TROUP. So we'll be moving from this place after all, is that what you mean, Jameson? Is that it?

JAMESON. Yes, old man. That's it.

TROUP. But what about me, what's he going to do about me? I told him, you see, I let him know that I'd seen him — oh why did I, why did I? Now he'll send me home to die in the jungle, or leave me here to perish by myself while you march on —

JAMESON. My dear old chap, there's no question of your being left, or of your being sent home, and certainly not of your dying. I do assure you.

TROUP. Oh, I shall die, Jameson, one way or the other. He'll see to that. Anyway I won't live without quinine, and he won't let me have any of Stanley's, that's how he'll do it —

JAMESON. But there's no need of Stanley's. I've got some. Here. (*He takes a phial out of his equipment.*) I've always kept some of my personal stock in reserve for my expeditions, in case I'm taken with a fever away from base — but I shan't need it now, shall I? Besides, I've never felt so well in my life.

TROUP. Oh, thank you, Jameson. Thank you. God bless you. God bless you. (*He bursts into tears.*) I'm sorry, I'm sorry — (*He sinks to his knees.*) Oh Jameson —

JAMESON *lifts* TROUP *up, holds him.*

BONNY. He should be in bed.

WARD. Well, why don't you put him there.

JAMESON. Yes, I'm sure you're the chap he needs —

BONNY. Yes, come along, old man, let's get you down. (*He puts his arm around* TROUP, *who is in a state of semi-collapse, and leads him off.*)

There is a pause.

WARD. Well. (*Smiling.*) You got back in the nick of time.

JAMESON. I've never moved so fast in my life. (*Little pause.*) How are you?

WARD. I'm anxious to hear about your adventures, what sort of chap is Tippu after all?

JAMESON. Oh very amusing. I kept storing away all sorts of things to tell you, (*going to the water bucket*) he goes in for a grand, not to say flamboyant style of hospitality, I've done one or two sketches of him in characteristic postures, I must show you later, by the way, oh, and I picked up a spectacular lizard and a butterfly I've never seen before, he fluttered over Tippu's head on my second morning and settled in a branch — (*Makes to pour himself water.*)

WARD. I'm afraid it's empty. John Henry being hors de combat, let me get you some.

JAMESON. No, no, I'm not really thirsty, I stopped for a drink when I came in. I wasn't thirsty then either, but one gets into the habit of taking a drink where one can as if it'll make up for the times one can't, which of course it doesn't. (*He laughs.*) But you haven't told me how you are?

WARD. All I can really say is that I'm no worse.

JAMESON. No worse?

WARD. Than the rest of us. I haven't been beating children senseless, for instance. But then that's the Major's way, not mine. Nor have I been stealing morphine from Stanley's supplies. But then that's Bonny's way, as it turns out.

JAMESON. Ah, I did wonder, before I left —

WARD. Troup's way you know about, as you caught the climax of his performance.

JAMESON. Yes, poor old Troup.

WARD. For my part, I've mainly lolled.

JAMESON. Lolled?

WARD. Yes, about and about, you know. Inflaming the

inflammable, goading the goadable and despising the despicable. That's been my way.

JAMESON. But I see you've made an attempt — (*Indicating the head of the woman.*)

WARD. Yesterday afternoon I dragged myself over to the river-bank, where I lolled in the hope of catching you in an early return. But all I saw were the corpses of two drowned niggers, rolled along by the sluggish current, and a few minutes later one nigger drowning. He sank some yards from me but bobbed up half an hour later, his head tangled in weeds, to be rolled off in his turn. I took him to be a deserting Zanzibari.

JAMESON. I'm sure there was nothing you could have done.

WARD. No, there wasn't, really.

JAMESON. Thank God you didn't go in after him. That current — you wouldn't have had a chance.

WARD. Not much of one, certainly.

JAMESON. So you mustn't reproach yourself.

WARD. Oh, I haven't been. Nor have I reproached myself for not reproaching myself, if you see.

JAMESON. Well I don't quite —

WARD. What I'm trying to say is, well, that given our different forms of degeneration, you were quite right to lie about seeing Tippu-Tib. False hope is probably our only hope now.

JAMESON. I didn't lie about seeing Tippu-Tib. I spent three days in his camp.

WARD. I see. Then you lied about what he said.

JAMESON. I reported him absolutely faithfully.

WARD. But you can't have believed him!

JAMESON (*after a pause*). Of course not. It was understood between us at once that his lies were a courtesy. Kindness, even, so that I shouldn't feel obliged to accuse him of treachery when hoplessly/ outnumbered. As I said, he's an excellent host, he really went to extravagant lengths to make me comfortable. (*Pause.*) I hoped you wouldn't be taken in. I shall need your support more than ever when the month is up and the doubts return.

WARD. And the whole process starts again. Although we shan't survive a whole year this time.

JAMESON. But if we can stretch the month into two and then three — until Stanley comes back, or we have news of his death. We have a chance. (*He smiles.*) At least we'll survive until tomorrow.

WARD. Of course if we were all like you, we could survive here for ever. And you could certainly survive without us, couldn't you?

JAMESON. Not quite. (*Pause.*) I say, would you like to have a look (*going to equipment*) at my rendering of Tippu, I think I've caught something of his —

WARD. No! No I wouldn't! (*Little pause.*) I'm sorry, I know it's infernally weak of me, I admire you more than any man I've ever met, and I'm flattered, flattered of course, that you should have counted on me for your support, even though I know you could manage without it, but it's just that — at the moment I wish — I wish you hadn't — no, that's not fair — I hadn't insisted on the truth. I'm sorry. Infernally weak. But then I am. I've learnt that much — (*He turns, goes towards the flap, stops, looks at* JAMESON.)

JAMESON. I'm sorry. If I'd realised —

WARD. Don't worry. You *can* count on me. For what I'm worth. (*He exits.*)

JAMESON *stands for a moment.*

From off, BARTTELOT's *voice, roaring out orders, and the sound of the Soudanese, and the Zanzibaris, calling to each other excitedly, coming near, then turning, going further off.*

JAMESON *goes to the doors, draws them almost closed, but allowing light to enter, comes back, stares at his equipment, then after a moment takes out a dead parakeet, gutted; then a small object, presumably the butterfly; looks at it; takes out several more objects, a bowl and a wooden spoon; finally his sketch pad and note-book. Opens the note-book, sits looking at it.*

JOHN HENRY *enters through the flap, limping bruised, carrying a water-bucket. He looks furtively over at* JAMESON, *who watches him go to replace the empty water-bucket with the full one, and then turn to go out.*

JAMESON. John Henry. John Henry — come here.

JOHN HENRY *comes over.*

Are you all right?

JOHN HENRY *nods.*

Well, you will be from now on. I promise you. No more bruises. No more. All right? (*He pats his head.*) Now you go and find your master, eh?

JOHN HENRY *nods, goes out through the flap.*

JAMESON *sits for a moment, looks at the sketches, then puts his face in his hands, as if tired. The voices off become less and less distinct. The lights fade slowly down to darkness.*

Scene Two

A couple of hours later.

    The set is in darkness. There comes from the darkness a low murmur, an exclamation, silence. Then another exclamation. BARTTELOT enters, left, carrying a lamp. JOHN HENRY is at his side. There is another exclamation. BARTTELOT goes over to the work desk, holds the lamp up. JAMESON is slumped over the desk, asleep. On the desk his note-book. His sketch-pad has fallen to the floor. BARTTELOT lights the lamp near the table, gives his own lamp to JOHN HENRY, who lights the other lamps.

    JAMESON groans heavily.

BARTTELOT (*stands looking down at him. Then puts a hand on JAMESON's shoulder.*) All right, Jamie. All right, old boy. It's only me.

    JAMESON lifts his head, sees BARTTELOT, lets out a cry of terror.

    Only me, Jamie. Only me.

JAMESON. Oh, I'm — I'm sorry.

BARTTELOT. A bad dream, eh?

JAMESON. Yes.

BARTTELOT. And are you properly awake now?

JAMESON. I'm not sure.

BARTTELOT. Well, I'm no dream, I can tell you. (*He laughs.*) I've had them on the march, up and down and around the

compound, then out into the jungle, making them walk, making
them feel their legs again, you see, the halt, the maim,
tomorrow I'll have the strongest moving with loads, some will
have to carry double when Tippu's lot arrive, we've lost so
many, but by God we won't lose another one, not another one
— John Henry — go and get some manioc — manioc, John
Henry — tell you the truth couldn't keep still myself, thinking
of his face — the expression on the devil's face.

JOHN HENRY *has gone out for the manioc.*

— when he finds every one of them intact, eh? Well, Mr
Stanley, what sort of year have you had? Let me tell you about
ours — oh, and here's our Mr Jameson, Mr Bonny, Mr Ward
and even Mr Troup, you do remember us, I take it, or had you
thought us dead, sir. Or deserted even? By God — by God —

JOHN HENRY *returns, pours the manioc.*

That's the boy, John Henry, keep off that bad leg, eh? (*He
drinks.*) Well, Jamie — and what about Emin Pasha, I thought
of him when I was marching them, first time for nearly a year
I remembered him. Make nonsense of the whole business if
Stanley hasn't got him out, if the Mahdi got to him first, eh?
All that we've been through because of Emin Pasha, and none
of it to do with him, just a battle between Stanley and
ourselves, and ourselves and the damned niggers, and ourselves
and ourselves, eh? (*He drinks, looks at* JAMESON.) But I'll tell
you something. He nearly won, old man. He did. If you hadn't
come back God knows what — Troup called me a lunatic and —
by God he was right. Because last night I committed the act of
a lunatic and Troup saw me at it. It was your Mrs Minchip who
drove me to it, on her drums, I sent John Henry out, and they
went silent, then started again, and — I couldn't endure it,
couldn't endure it, but I did, you see, instead of going out and
giving her a cuff myself I endured it, until the others had gone
to bed, and then I went out, walked over them, trampled on
them where they lay, or put my stick into their sides and stirred
them out of the way with the point, walking in a straight line
to their tent, and when I got there I went up to the woman
squatting there, beating away, and I grinned at her, you know
how my grin works, a grin and then a cuff, how they fold before
it, but this time not a bit of it, she kept on pounding away, not
even seeing me, and then I looked up, and there was his face
in the slit of their tent, peering out and grinning back at me,
and beneath that another slit, freshly cut, the barrel of his

rifle sticking out of it straight at me, right at my chest, you see,
and the woman pounding on, so I looked back at him, grinning
at his grin to wipe it off, and I could see him losing his nerve,
the barrel wavered, so I bent over the woman, you see, didn't
know what I was doing until my teeth were in her neck. Sank
them deep into her neck, to stop her on the drums at last. I
looked back at the slit and I thought now — now you nigger,
if you dare — with her blood still around my mouth, and I
laughed into his face. Laughed into his face with his woman's
blood around my mouth and his gun against my chest. It was a
good laugh, a good long laugh, all the time I was waiting for the
rifle to go off, thinking now, nigger, do it now — until I turned
and walked away, stepping on them again, on their arms and
legs and bellies and faces and when I got back to my tent I
remembered the blood was still around my mouth. I licked at
it with my tongue. Licked it off with my tongue. Drank some
manioc to get rid of the taste, and more manioc to keep the
dear old pater, you see, from watching his son lick up nigger
blood from around his mouth — or Stanley seeing — what I
had come to. And there was John Henry — and so he got the
brunt of it, poor little mite. Poor little mite. You see. Had to
tell you myself. Before you hear it from Troup. (*Pause.*) Well,
Jamie — what do you think of me now?

JAMESON. Why, exactly as I've always thought of you, old man.

BARTTELOT. You don't despise me for it.

JAMESON. No.

BARTTELOT. That's a relief. I care what you think of me, you
know. Always have. You, with your strength — well, you know
that. (*Pause.*) By God, you know, I may be the wrong man for
the Rear Column, that's why he chose me, but I did one good
thing, right at the beginning, I had the beating of Stanley right
at the beginning, when I made him give you over to me.

JAMESON. Give me over to you?

BARTTELOT. One of Parke, Jephson or Stair will remain behind
with you, Barttelot, he said. You may choose. And I said,
None of them, thank you, Mr Stanley, the man I want is
Jameson. Jameson, Jameson, he said, but Jameson isn't an
officer, he's a paying gentleman. And I said, It's Jameson I
want, Mr Stanley. And he gave me a Stanley look, and I
readied myself for a row, instead he whinnied out some
laughter, Very well, he said. Very well. But I advise you,

Major Barttelot, for the sake of harmony between you, not
to tell him he's staying behind at your request. Even Jameson,
gentleman though he is, might come to hate you for it. Stanley,
the great judge of men! Didn't know you as I knew you, even
then — and that's where I had the beating of him. And beaten
him all over again by telling you. Although I've waited until
today to do it, I admit, and probably wouldn't have today if —
if —

JAMESON. Fate hadn't worked things otherwise.

BARTTELOT. That's it, old man! That's it!

JAMESON. But then fate, being fate, never does. At least in as
much as you've been mine, and didn't.

BARTTELOT. All I can say is, in spite of everything, I wouldn't
have had it different.

JAMESON. Amen to that!

BONNY *enters through the flap.*

Ah, Bonny, here you are then — Jameson and I were just
having a glass — John Henry, a glass for Mr Bonny —

JOHN HENRY *pours* BONNY *a glass.*

Off, the drums start, with a flourish.

BARTTELOT. There they go, eh Jamie? So that's all right then —
well, they've something to celebrate tonight, John Henry, go
tell them with the Major's compliments that tonight they
may play their drums — but low, tell them — low.

BONNY (*meanwhile, spotting* JAMESON's *fallen sketch-pad,
picks it up*). Brought back some drawings too, eh?

JAMESON. Yes.

BONNY. So quite a successful trip, what with one thing and the
other.

JOHN HENRY *goes out.*

BONNY (*looking through the pad*). Any of Tippu-Tib?

BARTTELOT. What, Tippu, I must have a look at those, get to
know the devil on different terms, eh? By God, it'll be hard to
keep a check on my tongue when he comes in here — How
d'you do, Mr Tib, glad to make your acquaintance at last, sir —

WARD *enters through the flap.*

Ah, here you are, Ward — here's a glass of Yambuya

champagne for you – and *I've* got good news – fish stew
tonight.

BONNY. What?

BARTTELOT (*laughs*). No, it's all right, Bonny, three I picked
up down-river when I was marching the men, not the rotting
pair this morning – Jamie, you haven't heard about that yet,
Bonny and I caught ourselves a woman yesterday, hobbled her,
brought her back, her man came in this morning with two
stinking fish –

The drums have quietened.

TROUP *enters through the flap.*

Troup, by God, you've come – here – a glass for Troup – but
should you be up, even for Yambuya champagne, old man –
here – (*pouring him a glass*) should you be?

TROUP. Thank you. Jameson's quinine, you know – (*He clears
his throat.*) Um Major, I want to say – say before everybody
– that – I said some things this morning I – I deeply regret,
accused you of all sorts of nonsense, which Bonny tells me – I
realise was just – just delirium –

BARTTELOT (*pause*). Well – you and I have had our – our –
what's passed is passed, eh? That's the thing – let's drink
instead – drink to, to –

WARD. Tippu-Tib. (*He glances at* JAMESON.)

BARTTELOT. Why, yes – Tippu-Tib, damn his soul!

REST. Tippu-Tib, damn his soul!

BONNY. I saw him a minute ago, yes, here he is – (*Flicking
open the sketch pad.*)

BARTTELOT. What, let's see, why that's as good as your famous
A Faithful Zanzibari says his Farewell, Jamie – what slyness,
what pomp, eh, and his rifle – the one Stanley gave him –
over his chest – hah, hah, hah!

JAMESON *puts his hand to his forehead.*

BARTTELOT *goes to get the manioc jug.*

WARD (*to* JAMESON). Are you all right?

JAMESON. Yes, yes – just a touch tired –

BONNY *is casually turning over pages of the pad.*

TROUP (*to* JAMESON). I'm very conscious of my debt to you, Jameson. For the quinine — and everything else.

JAMESON. Oh.

JOHN HENRY *enters.*

BARTTELOT. Ah, there's a good boy — well done John Henry, well done — (*Coming back with the jug.*)

BONNY (*lets out an exclamation*). What's this?

JAMESON (*looking up*). Mmmm?

WARD *saunters over to look.*

BARTTELOT *comes over with the jug, offers to pour for* TROUP.

TROUP. No thank you, Major, feeling a bit — a bit — (*Goes, sits down.*)

BONNY. A little girl tied to a tree.

JAMESON. Oh. (*Little pause.*) Yes.

BARTTELOT *comes over, looks over* BONNY's *other shoulder.*

BARTTELOT. What, what is it, Jamie?

BONNY *turns another page, stares at it.* WARD, BARTTELOT *also stare.*

WARD. But she's — they're —

BARTTELOT. Can't make it out, what's going on?

There is a pause.

JAMESON. It's a cannibal feast. (*Pause.*) I happened to mention to Tippu that once or twice I'd come across the remains of one, but never the beginnings or middle of one. So the next morning he invited me to accompany him and some of his chaps to a village where a couple of Tippu's men had been doing a bit of slaving. Among their merchandise was a girl of about thirteen, I suppose — that girl. I bought her from them, at Tippu's suggestion, for five brass-rods, and then we took her off to a cannibal chief Tippu knew of, who was told he could have her for lunch on the understanding that I did drawings of him while he was at it, and Tippu got a goat for our supper. (*Pause.*) To my knowledge it's the first time the whole process has been recorded. (*Pause.*) He was my host.

WARD. You bought the girl, then watched her being killed and prepared for the pot and cooked and eaten. And made sketches of it?

BONNY. And here, asleep under a tree, that's him is it, afterwards?

JAMESON. Yes.

BARTTELOT (*quietly*). What have you done?

JAMESON. What? (*He looks around at their faces.*) Nothing very terrible, surely. The girl had already been caught by slavers, she was bound to end up in the pot — they have no other use for them at that age. Good Heavens, we've flogged them to death, we've watched them die by the score, what does it matter, one nigger girl — (*He stops, looks at* WARD.)
Yes. I see. I suppose I've slightly lost my — my — My curiosity and the uniqueness of it evidently blinded me to the — the — (*stops*) I'm sorry.

BONNY. Tippu-Tib doesn't have any of these, by any chance, does he?

JAMESON. Some rough versions, yes.

BONNY. Did you sign them for him?

JAMESON. Yes.

BARTTELOT. Do you know — do you know — what he'll do with them? Why, he'll head straight back to the Falls and show them — show them around to everyone, everyone. The story will be all over the Congo, in England, in London, on the first steamer — that we participated — participated in a cannibal — a cannibal —

BONNY. They'll say you ate your share of her, too.

BARTTELOT. All these months — this year — of waiting and hoping — and then just as the end is in sight you — you — with your damned — your damned — collection — you bring us down!

The drums increase, and increase, through BARTTELOT's *next speech, almost drowning it towards its end.*

Why, it's all been for nothing, nothing! Worse than nothing, to dishonour, to disgrace — by God man, after all this you've destroyed us, worse than death, worse than desertion, in England, with Stanley, here, destroyed — destroyed — is that why Stanley gave you to me, because he knew, he knew you'd — you'd — (*he is shaking, as if in a fit*) do his work for him, you and Stanley, is that what it was, — (*he holds his stick towards* JAMESON, *makes as if to thrust it into him, then wheels around, sees* JOHN HENRY) I told you — I told you to stop them, told you, (*gouges the stick into* JOHN HENRY) little black — scum — scum — (*as the pounding of the drum is at its fullest pitch*)

WARD *runs over to stop* BARTTELOT.

BARTTELOT *shakes him off savagely, then rounds on him raises his stick, makes to thrust it into* WARD, *then turns, flings open the doors, on the darkness, with fires burning, drums pounding, strides off.*

BONNY *goes over to the door, stares out.*

WARD *goes to* JOHN HENRY, *bends over him, then straightens.*

TROUP *is sitting, motionless.*

JAMESON *is sitting, motionless.*

The drums stop, There is silence.

BARTTELOT (*off*). Hah, hah, hah, hah! Hah, hah, hah —

There is a shot.

Silence.

WARD *moves towards the doors.*

There are sudden cries, shouts, off.

BONNY *pushes the doors closed before* WARD *reaches them, locks them. Turns his back to them.*

BONNY. If you go out there they'll do the same to you. And then come on in and do the same to us. (*Pause.*) We'll get him in the morning.

WARD *hesitates, then turns away. Looks at* JAMESON. *He goes over to him, looks at him.*

JAMESON *looks slowly up at* WARD.

There is a pause.

TROUP (*in a dull voice*). Now perhaps you'll listen to me. Now perhaps we can go home.

BONNY *goes over, helps himself to manioc from the jug.*

WARD *puts his hand on* JAMESON's *shoulder.*

Go home at last, eh?

BONNY *drinks.*

*Lights fade slowly on this tableau, to darkness, as the drums
start up again excitable, unrhythmic.*
The same. Some days later.
   *The doors are slightly open. From off, the sound of voices,
Zanzibari, Soudanese. BONNY is moving about, doing an
inventory of the boxes, but slowly. The sound of STANLEY's
voice, off, commanding. BONNY straightens, listens.*
   STANLEY *enters through the doors, pulling them wide.*

STANLEY. Well Bonny, Parke is back from the Falls, with
   some news. He spoke to Mr Troup, who is in excellent health,
   and has booked his passage back to Southampton. He is also
   in excellent voice. His self-justifications and denials have fuelled
   the scandal, God knows what form the story will finally take
   when it appears in *The Times*, but it will certainly have
   precedence with the public over my own poor efforts, who
   will want to read of the successful relief of Emin Pasha when
   there are tales of Barttelot's lash and Jameson's experiments
   in slaughtering, cooking and consuming infant girls to wallow
   in, eh? Mr Jameson, by the way, is dead.

BONNY. Oh.

STANLEY. He died at a Mission House between here and the
   Falls. He went too fast, in no state to travel, though if he'd
   had quinine with him he would probably have survived, why
   he didn't have quinine is another of the incomprehensible — as
   there is quinine here — is there not? But let us be charitable
   and assume that his neglect of himself had something
   Roman in it. If not Roman, then at least English. He was
   buried by Mr Ward, some nonsense about a Union Jack
   draped over a coffin rough-hewn from a tree — no doubt a
   bugle carved on the spot to sound a lament, eh? Pshaw! The
   good people at the Mission were much moved, being
   ignorant at the time that they were officiating over the
   remains of a celebrated cannibal, with his good friend, the
   opium fiend.

BONNY. I can't be sure it was Mr Ward who took the laudanum —
   all I know is that some is missing —

STANLEY (*looks at him*). Mr Ward left the Mission House, and
   has completely vanished. You, on the other hand, Bonny, are
   here, the only survivor, in the moral sense, of the Yambuya

fiasco. So let us make sure that your reputation is unsullied, eh?

BONNY. Thank you, sir. I felt somebody had to stay behind until you —

STANLEY. I'm not interested in your motives, Bonny. One can't plan motives only results. But there's no way of planning for gentlemen like Jameson, or a maniac like Barttelot. I did my best. I knew him to be a danger to us all, that's why I left him behind, in this place, where he could do no harm. (*Laughs.*) With an English gentleman to keep a check on him. And a set of orders that couldn't have been simpler, clearer or more flexible. All he had to do was to follow my orders. Easy enough, easy enough, even for a maniac, eh?

BONNY. At least you rescued Emin Pasha.

STANLEY. Who resents it bitterly, being comfortable and probably safe where he was. By the way, Bonny, where did you bury my John Henry?

BONNY. Outside the compound, with all the other — um —

STANLEY *looks at him, then bends, begins to pull off one of his boots.*

BONNY *waits.*

STANLEY. Be so kind as to take those damned turtles to the kitchen, would you?

BONNY *releases the turtles, takes them out through the flap.*

STANLEY *straightens for a moment, then begins to take off the other boot.*

Curtain.

MOLLY

Author's Note

Molly is an adaptation for the stage of the earliest of my
television plays — *Death of a Teddy Bear* — which was written for
BBC's Wednesday Play about ten years ago. Brenda Bruce, Hywel
Bennet, Rachel Kempson and the late Kenneth J. Warren played
the original Molly, Oliver, Eve and Teddy; Warris Hussein was our
director; Kenith Trodd the producer; and Gerald Savory wiped
the tape.

The source of *Death of a Teddy Bear* was the Alma Rattenbury
case, an account of which I came across in a paperback called (I
think) *Ten Famous Trials*, left discarded in a railway compartment.
I was on my way from London to Cambridge to supervise Trinity
undergraduates in (probably) Hobbes, or Hume, or Aeschylus or
some such, and had a briefcase full of essays to mark. I flicked
through the pages of the paperback — it was stained and swollen
as if a dog had urinated over it — in the cursory manner of one
who has something of more consequence on his mind, plucked
out a handful of essays, and settled down to the book. When I
arrived at Cambridge I left the book where I'd found it, but for
the rest of that day, and for many subsequent days and
(especially) nights, I was haunted by Mrs Rattenbury's story — or
what of it I could perceive behind the dozen pages or so in which
her trial had been described. So when Kenith Trodd asked me if
I'd like to try my hand at a full-length television play, the subject
was already fully there, and at least partially shaped, even though
unwritten. Which is perhaps why I didn't go back to Mrs
Rattenbury herself, neither to her trial nor to reconstructions of
the crime. I based my play on the effect that the dozen pages had
had on me (the specifics being pretty well forgotten), changed the
names, and hoped that my sense of the drama would find its own
form. *Death of a Teddy Bear* was not, therefore, *about* Mrs
Rattenbury and the murder in which she was involved, although
of course without her it would never have been written.

I felt strongly enough about *Death of a Teddy Bear* not to

want to lose it to television — not realising then that the BBC, after showing it twice, was simply going to chuck it away (see The New Review Vol. 3 No. 27) — and about five years ago I wrote the first stage draft. I followed as closely as I could the emotional line and the basic structure of the original, extending some scenes and subtracting those that depended on the mobility of the camera, and so inevitably, and against my intentions, altered the tone of the whole. Further drafts altered further, and I might have left the final draft in a drawer if it hadn't been for the discovery that the television version no longer exists. So in a sense its recent production (at the New Spoleto Festival, in Charleston, last Spring) and its present slightly different (slightly re-written) production (at the Watford Palace Theatre) and its publication in *The New Review* must be attributed to 'Wiper' Savory, who left me with no alternative but to preserve the play in the only form now left.

N.B. Terence Rattigan's play, *Cause Celebre*, now on in the West End, is also based on the Rattenbury case. I haven't seen it, but gather that it started life as a radio play a couple of years back, and unlike *Molly*, concentrates on the trial. I believe there have been other Rattenbury plays, but have no details of them.

MOLLY was first presented in Britain in November 1977 at the Watford Palace Theatre, with the following cast:

MOLLY	Mary Miller
TEDDY	Raymond Francis
OLIVER	Anthony Allen
EVE	Barbara Atkinson
GREAVES	Arthur Cox
POLICE CONSTABLE	Stephen Enns

Directed by Stephen Hollis
Set design by Christopher Morley
Costume design by Ann Curtis
Lighting by Brian Harris

Act One

Scene One

The play is set in the 1930s.

    Living-room of a house. It has three doors: one stage right, which leads into the conservatory, part of which is visible on the stage; one back, that leads into the kitchen, dining-room etc; and one left, that leads to the hall, front door, and other offices and stairs. In the room is a cocktail cabinet, new and of the Thirties, amply stocket; an arm-chair; a large sofa; tables, chairs, all in the style of the Twenties and Thirties.

    The curtain rises on the room, empty. Light beginning to fade. There is a pause, and then MOLLY, wearing a light coat, a silk scarf, enters slowly through the conservatory. She takes off her scarf, drops it onto the sofa. She stands listless, then takes from her coat pocket her cigarettes and a lighter. She lights a cigarette, draws on it deeply, then stares around her with an air of desperation, goes to radio, turns it on, listens for a moment to music, makes an irritated expression, turns the radio off, goes to drinks table, pours herself a drink, takes a sip as, above, sound of door opening.

TEDDY (*off, up*). Moll! (*Calling.*) Molly!

MOLLY (*hesitates*). In here darling.

    There is another call of MOLL, then a door slams. The sound of footsteps, coming down. MOLLY puts down glass, walks swiftly out through the conservatory, vanishing exactly as the door, left, opens and TEDDY enters, saying irritably MOLL as he does so. Sees the room empty, makes an irritable exclamation goes over to the conservatory, shouts MOLL! He is in his mid-sixties, has a deaf aid, elaborate and visible and of the Thirties, and an air of slightly bogus physicality. Shouts again. MOLL-LY

EVE *enters from the back. Looks toward the conservatory. She is a woman in her mid-fifties, severely dressed and severe of expression; spectacles; and an air of brisk efficiency.*

TEDDY (*off*). Damn it! (*He comes back from the conservatory, sees EVE.*) Oh, hello Evie, where's Moll?

EVE (*speaking loudly*). She's gone for a walk.

TEDDY. When?

EVE. About an hour ago.

TEDDY. Then why didn't she ask me. (*Goes to cocktail cabinet.*) I could have just done with a walk.

EVE. You were taking a nap.

TEDDY. But I didn't want to. I wanted to go for a walk. I spend the whole afternoon waiting for her to make up her mind whether she wants to go or not —

Pours himself a large Scotch.
EVE *sees MOLLY's scarf, goes over to it and deftly and surreptitiously picks it up, and puts it on one of the tables, where it is unlikely to be noticed.*

and then I go upstairs to get a book and sit down on the bed with it for a moment and — (*Adds soda water to his Scotch, splashes it.*) Damn, damn! (*Looks at EVE.*)

EVE. I'll get a cloth —

TEDDY. Oh sit down Evie, sit down. I can manage — (*Mops up the soda with a handkerchief.*) Sorry Eve, I'm always a grump if I doze through the afternoon — like a bear with a headache — what'll you have, one of your dry as dust sherrys?

EVE. Oh, no thank you, Teddy, I really ought to get back to the kitchen —

TEDDY (*pours EVE a sherry*). Tell me, Evie, do you think Moll wants to stay. We've been here a month now but she makes me feel as if we only just moved in yesterday, or we've going to be moved out tomorrow, but we're never going to have the part in between, has she said anything to you? (*Brings her the sherry.*)

EVE. Thank you. Well, she's said she likes it here.

TEDDY. What about you?

EVE. Oh yes. Very much.

TEDDY. That's good, because we need you, Evie. Your
   hitching on to us was real luck, you keep us orderly. Don't
   you think of abandoning us.

EVE. That's very kind of you, Teddy.

TEDDY. Well, it's her England, that's what she said she wanted.
   And it'd do for me if she settles for it. Wish I didn't sleep so
   much, that's the only thing. Never slept like this in Canada.
   Never had time to. But then I had a business to run, bills of
   lading to get out, had to meet the ships at sometimes two in
   the morning, did you know that, Evie? (*Pause.*) Funny thing is
   I miss the smell of fish. The whole town smelt of it, the
   uptown streets, it got into the stores. I didn't notice it until I'd
   left. Hey, it's getting dark. That's something else I'm not used
   to, your English springs. We don't have springs in Canada, just
   a sort of wink between winter and summer. But then we have
   our falls, you don't have falls, do you?

EVE. No, we only have autumns, I'm afraid.

TEDDY. What? Well, I don't like her out in the dark. Wandering
   about. She used to tell me England's got the best climate in the
   world, you know what I think now I've seen it, it may be the
   best climate, but the weather's terrible. (*Laughs.*) Not my idea
   of friendly either. (*Goes back to cocktail cabinet.*) Now in
   Nova Scotia, move into a village they'd be right round asking
   what they could do to help, inviting us over, but we've been
   here two whole weeks, and who do we know, Dr Gracey, when
   I need him to look after my ears.

EVE. More people know Tom Fool than Tom Fool knows people.

TEDDY. Who?

EVE. Tom Fool.

TEDDY. Tom who?

EVE. Fool.

TEDDY. Well I don't know him, somebody in the village?

EVE. It's a saying.

TEDDY (*not having understood*). Oh. Ready for another?
   (*Coming across with the bottle.*)

EVE. No I won't, thanks —

   TEDDY *pours sherry.* EVE *just manages to catch it.*

TEDDY. You know what woke me up? I thought I heard her

singing, that one about the seals of Nanaimo, and playing the
piano — I heard it quite clear, every note, so it must have been
a dream — she was going to try and write more songs once she
got back here, that's why she wanted a place with a piano in it,
but she hasn't played it yet — I'm going to get on to her about
that, this evening. Did you know I got that seal song played
over Station RCVX — knew the owner — he put it out across
the whole of Nova Scotia. Bob Hoskins. He was a good friend
of mine. In hardware. You ever been married, Evie?

EVE. No.

TEDDY. Why not?

EVE. I'm afraid no one ever asked me.

TEDDY. That's the girl. (*Laughs.*) Hey, Evie, mind if I ask you a
delicate question?

EVE. No.

TEDDY. You sure?

EVE. Well, as I'm living in your house, you have a perfect right
to know anything about me you want. Within reason, of
course.

TEDDY. Am I paying you enough?

EVE. Yes, quite enough, thank you, Teddy. No thank you. You're
more than generous. Now if you'll excuse me I really must go
and have a look at the dinner. (*Gets up and goes out.*)

TEDDY. Oh.

*Sits for a moment, then gets up, goes to the cocktail cabinet,
adds a dash of Scotch, squirts soda water, splashes it slightly,
makes as if to mop it, gestures irritably, goes over to the
conservatory, stands looking through.*

What the hell's she playing at?

There is a ring at the door-bell, left. TEDDY *makes no move.*

EVE (*appears from back*). Somebody at the door.

TEDDY still makes no move. EVE *makes to speak again,
instead goes off, left.*

TEDDY (*turns, walks to the door, back, stands at it*). Hey Evie,
I'm getting really worried —

EVE re-enters from left, accompanied by OLIVER.
OLIVER *is a boy of about seventeen, awkward and not
particularly attractive. Dressed in his Sunday clothes, as for an
interview.*

TEDDY *turns away from the door, sees* OLIVER *and* EVE.

EVE (*coming over to* TEDDY), It's a boy from the village.

TEDDY. What? Is Moll all right?

EVE. He says something about a job.

TEDDY. What job?

EVE. I've no idea.

TEDDY (*goes over to* OLIVER). Well hello boy, what can we do for you?

OLIVER. Sir. They said at Sprinkley's there was a job.

EVE. That's the garage in the village.

TEDDY. What's your name, boy?

OLIVER. Oliver, sir.

TEDDY. What?

OLIVER. Oliver, sir. Oliver Treefe.

TEDDY. Oliver?

OLIVER. Yes sir.

TEDDY. Oliver what, Oliver?

OLIVER. Oliver Treefe, sir.

EVE. You'll have to speak up please, Oliver.

TEDDY. Sorry Oliver, I'm not picking you up.

OLIVER (*realising*). OLIVER TREEFE, SIR. (*In a bellow.*)

TEDDY. Oliver Treefsir, well Oliver Treefsir, what can we do for you?

OLIVER. They said (*in a bellow*) at Sprinkley's Garage a lady had been in to inquire about a boy, sir.

EVE (*to* TEDDY). It must have been Molly. (*To* OLIVER.) When did she come in?

OLIVER. This afternoon (*bellowing at* EVE) they said. They said she said there was a car needed looking after. Mr Goldberg's Alvis.

TEDDY. What?

EVE. Mr Goldberg's Alvis, Teddy.

TEDDY. Mr Goldberg hasn't got an Alvis. I've got it. Part of the deal for the house. He left it for me for what he called a consideration, he's probably bought himself a new car out of the consideration, eh boy? Quite a business man, your Mr Goldberg. (*Laughs*.)

OLIVER *laughs*.

TEDDY. Quite a businessman. It doesn't go, boy. Needs a lot of tinkering. Can you tinker?

OLIVER. Yes sir.

TEDDY. Can, eh? That's right, don't undersell yourself, what about a drink, we got some of that stuff you English call beer somewhere and you look to be at the beer-guzzling age, eh Evie? Like one? (*Goes to cocktail cabinet*.)

OLIVER. Well, no thank you very much sir.

TEDDY *begins to wrestle with a bottle of beer*.

EVE. Did the lady mention any special time to call, Oliver?

OLIVER. They said she said the evening would be best, Missus.

EVE. I see. And was it only about the car?

OLIVER. Well, they said she said it would be a bit of driving and helping about the garden and odd-jobs. They said it was a proper job, Missus.

EVE. Well, I'm afraid Mrs Treadley isn't here at the moment, but I'll take down your details and let her have them. Who can give you references, Oliver?

OLIVER. Well, there's Sprinkley's.

EVE. And anyone else?

TEDDY (*pours beer, which foams up over cabinet*). Damn! (*Mops at it with handkerchief*.) First thing you've got to do is make her go, second thing is to break me into her ways. I'm not used to cars like your Mr Goldberg's Alvises, especially now my balance's gone, so you'll have to show me how to handle her, whether she needs coaxing or bullying, a car's like any machine, a man's made her so she's going to have something wrong with her. I used to do a lot of driving — ever heard of the Breton Trail, that's in Nova Scotia. (*Bringing* OLIVER *his beer*.) Here, get yourself outside of that —

OLIVER. Thank you sir.

TEDDY. That's in Nova Scotia, where the roads go straight ten

yards before they turn around and go back five. In a Manson.
By God I loved that car. Always knew where to tinker when
she gave me trouble. Think I could get to love a car that used
to belong to your Mr Goldberg, eh, that he left to rot and rust
for a consideration? Eh?

EVE. I was just getting down some references, Teddy.

TEDDY. Oh.

EVE. Now who else besides Sprinkley's, Oliver?

OLIVER. I done some gardening with my Dad —

TEDDY. Who?

OLIVER. My dad, sir.

TEDDY. Your Dad — a reference from your Dad? We could all
get references from our Dads, boy. (*Laughs.*)

OLIVER. No, I only meant —

EVE. Where else have you worked, Oliver?

MOLLY *enters the conservatory, stands watching for a
moment, unseen by the others.*

EVE. Where else have you worked, Oliver?

OLIVER. Well — (*Pauses.*) — well I did some for Mrs Shepherd,
Missus, but I stopped after a bit.

EVE. Indeed, why?

MOLLY (*enters*). Of course, you're the boy, aren't you, that
Sprinkley's promised to send. I'm so sorry I wasn't here when
you arrived, please forgive me.

OLIVER. That's all right, Miss.

MOLLY (*to* TEDDY *and* EVE). I popped in as I was passing the
garage, when the thought struck, and then it slipped my mind,
sorry darlings.

TEDDY. Where you been, Moll, old Evie was getting worried
about you, out there in the dark.

MOLLY (*to* EVE). Were you, darling? There was no need, it was
all quite friendly and above board. Well, what have you fixed
up, between the three of you?

EVE. We're just sorting out the question of references.

TEDDY. Drink, Moll. (*Going to cocktail cabinet.*)

MOLLY. Thank you, darling, I'd love one.

TEDDY. We've just been trying to make out from your Oliver Treefsir here whether he's the sort that kills us.

MOLLY (*smiling at* OLIVER). Are you the sort to kill us, Oliver?

OLIVER. No, Miss.

MOLLY. There we are, what more could we ask. You see, my husband's the sort that likes to drive very fast himself, but when he's being driven he likes it to be by the sort that drives very slow, don't you darling? But I can't drive at all, so I like everybody to drive fast, even the people in other cars.

TEDDY *comes over, hands* MOLLY *a drink.*

MOLLY. Thank you, darling. Now what about the gardening, are you going to do that for us too?

OLIVER. Well, yes Miss, I mean if you want —

MOLLY. Because we need a gardener to garden for us as well as a driver who won't kill us, Oliver, it's all in the most terrible tangle out there, some of the spring whatsits look quite alarming. What are your fingers like, can we see them?

OLIVER. Miss?

MOLLY. Can we see your fingers? (OLIVER *shows his fingers.*) Mmmm — yes, they look as if they could be green, you see we met a lady on the boat coming over from Canada who talked every lunch time and dinner time about gardening, and she said — do you remember, darling? —

TEDDY. What?

MOLLY. The herbaceous border lady, darling, she said that for gardens green fingers were quite essential, of course, and that the best way to make flowers grow was to talk to them and sing to them and even to recite poems to them, now would you be willing to talk and sing and recite poems to our flowers, Oliver? (*Looks at him seriously.*)

OLIVER. Um, well — (*Gives a little laugh.*)

MOLLY. Oh well (*smiling*). What about pulling up weeds and mowing the lawn instead?

OLIVER. Oh yes, Miss. I could do that. I mean, my Dad does the gardening for some of them in the village in the evenings, and I've helped him.

MOLLY. There you are then. You meet our requirements exactly, doesn't he darling?

TEDDY. What?

EVE. Excuse me, Moll, but I haven't quite found out how you can get hold of Mrs Shepherd.

MOLLY. Why do I want to get hold of Mrs Shepherd?

TEDDY. Hey, that boy's been standing there with a mitt full of beer and you ladies haven't let him take a sip of it — you have your drink, boy. Go on.

OLIVER *hesitates, then raises his glass, drinks.*

EVE (*to* MOLLY). Oliver used to work for Mrs Shepherd until she let him go.

OLIVER *finishes his drink.*

TEDDY. That's the boy!

MOLLY. Why did Mrs Shepherd let you go, Oliver?

OLIVER. She — well, she just said she didn't need me any more, that's all.

MOLLY. Oh. And if she had needed you any more we wouldn't be able to have you now, would we, so you see, Evie, Mrs Shepherd was only acting for the best, wasn't she Oliver, if we *can* have you now, that is? But omigod, how much are we to pay you?

OLIVER. Well, Miss, whatever — I don't know.

MOLLY. How much did Mrs Shepherd pay you?

OLIVER. Two pound a week, Miss.

MOLLY. Two pounds a week!

EVE. That would be the normal rate.

MOLLY. But it seems a mere trifle for chauffeuring us about and not killing us and keeping out weeds down and our flowers up and general handymanning, you would do a little handymanning wouldn't you, Oliver? I really think a minimum of four pounds a week, wouldn't you, darling?

EVE. Four pounds!

TEDDY. What?

MOLLY. Four pounds a week for Oliver, darling, includes handymanning.

TEDDY. Give him four and a half.

MOLLY. Four pounds ten, Oliver, there we are. Will you come to us for that?

OLIVER. Yes Miss! I mean, I'll have to talk it over with my Dad —

MOLLY. Of course you will. But even so, I think we've got you, haven't we?

OLIVER. Yes Miss.

MOLLY. Well then, Dad willing, when can you start, tomorrow?

EVE. Tomorrow's Sunday.

MOLLY. Monday then.

OLIVER. Yes Miss.

MOLLY. All settled darling, I had to use my wiles but I've brought him to it.

TEDDY. Another beer, boy?

OLIVER. Um, no thanks —

MOLLY. Oh, we mustn't keep him any longer (*taking the glass from* OLIVER, *winks at him*) he's got important matters to discuss with his Dad. Haven't you?

OLIVER. Yes Miss.

EVE. I'll see you out, Oliver. (*Leads him to the door.*)

MOLLY. See you Monday, Oliver.

TEDDY. 'Bye there, boy.

OLIVER. Sir. (*Shouting.*)

TEDDY. I like the look of him.

MOLLY. Did you really, darling? Can't say I did, pale, spotty and slightly furtive, I thought. But just the sort to know all about engines and lawn-mowers and things — (*taking off her coat*) and one never does know how to turn people down — (*Drops coat in chair.*)

TEDDY. Where did you go?

MOLLY. Further than I meant.

TEDDY (*sits down, looks at her*). Why didn't you take me with you?

MOLLY (*goes over to him, rumples his hair*). You were snoozing, my sweet, I hadn't the heart to wake you — (*kisses the top of his head, goes over to the cocktail cabinet with his glass, pours them both a drink*) — and it really wasn't very nice anyway, you'd have found me a terrible bore. I kept thinking I heard a tune I could write down and make into one of my silly songs, it was as if I were following it, through one field, then another, right to the river where the bridge is, I was sure it was there somewhere, like a person I was going to meet, but nobody came (*brings him his drink back*) nobody at all.

TEDDY. What? I missed all that.

MOLLY. I was just chattering.

EVE *enters, from left.*

MOLLY. Well darling, you got it all out of him, I take it.

EVE. What?

MOLLY. Mrs What'sit's address and the rest of it.

EVE. Mrs Shepherd's. Yes, I did. I hope you don't mind. I think she might be that lady we saw in the Post Office the other day, having a parcel weighed.

MOLLY. With a ridiculous hat and false teeth?

EVE. I didn't really notice her teeth.

MOLLY. What about her ankles, did you notice those?

EVE. Notice what?

MOLLY. Weren't they very thick?

EVE. I'm afraid I didn't notice her ankles, either.

MOLLY. Then it can't have been Mrs What'sit, darling, in the Post Office.

EVE. You've met her then?

MOLLY. Who?

EVE. Mrs Shepherd.

TEDDY. Who are you two nattering about?

MOLLY. Mrs Shepherd, darling.

TEDDY. Who's she?

MOLLY. We haven't the slightest idea, but Eve's got her address and she's determined to find out, aren't you, darling?

EVE. I'm sorry, Molly, I know it wasn't my place to interfere —

MOLLY. Oh Eve!

EVE. It's just that I don't think you should take people on
without knowing anything about them, except what they tell
you themselves.

MOLLY. Really, darling? I don't agree, we took you on without
knowing anything about you except what you told us yourself,
and that's worked out quite well.

EVE. I gave you three references!

MOLLY. Yes, darling but you don't think I read them. They were
far too long, and bound to be flattering, which wouldn't
have been fun, so I hired you in lieu.

EVE *picks up* MOLLY's *coat and scarf, takes them out to hall,
left.*

MOLLY. Omigod! (*Sinks into a chair.*)

TEDDY. What?

MOLLY. I've offended Eve again.

TEDDY. What?

MOLLY. She really is the most humourless —

EVE *enters, from left.*

TEDDY (*not seeing her*). When's she going to feed us, that's what
I want to know.

EVE. I'm on my way to the kitchen now.

MOLLY. Oh darling — (*to* EVE) I was only teasing, of course I
read your references, they were divine, one from the two ladies
in Richmond, one from the Doctor in Kingston and one from
— from — wherever, but I remember it quite well, said you
were scrupulous in violet ink and couldn't manage without
you and no more could we, and you were right to insist on
Mr What'sit's address, and I did rush us into the youth quite
fecklessly, it was just that I felt funny about having forgotten
him entirely, but I know he won't get away with anything,
darling, with you to keep an eye on him, and if you ever bump
into Mrs Shepherd again you can quiz her to your heart's
content, all right, darling, all forgiven? Please. Pretty please
with sugar on it?

EVE (*smiles*). Oh Moll. Now you're teasing me again.

MOLLY. No I'm not, darling. I mean it. Every word almost.

EVE (*still smiling*). It'll just be a few minutes, Teddy.

TEDDY. No rush, Evie, have another drink!

EVE. Then you'll never eat. (*Goes out back.*)

MOLLY. Omigod! (*Wearily. Lights a cigarette.*)

    TEDDY *watches her. There is a pause.*

TEDDY. Hey you, come here! (*Pause.*) Come on, come here, I said.

MOLLY (*concealing irritation, clearly knows what is to happen, gets up, goes over to* TEDDY). Sir?

TEDDY. Now my girl, how many's that since lunch?

MOLLY. Only one, sir.

TEDDY. Come on, Moll, the truth now. All the time you were gadding about out there.

MOLLY. Well, three. (*Pause.*) Four. (*Pause. Holds up five fingers.*) Ten. Twenty.

TEDDY (*not hearing*). Five, eh? Well, add on another four and one on top of that makes — one — two — three — four — five — six — seven — eight — nine — (*Slapping* MOLLY *on the bottom, laughing.*)

    MOLLY *giggles, cries ouch.*

TEDDY. Now get us another drink, girl.

MOLLY. My Lord.

    Makes a little curtsey, takes his glass, pours him a drink and one for herself.

TEDDY. And another thing, girl, what about getting to the piano, all your talk about your songs and you haven't touched a key since we moved in, that was another of Mr Goldberg's considerations — he can hire himself a whole band out of that one — I was telling Eve all about your seal-song and Bob Hoskins transmitting it over RCVX — (*takes her hand as she brings him the drink*) play it now, eh, Moll.

MOLLY. But darling, she's getting the dinner on the table.

TEDDY. What? Don't want to?

MOLLY. Not very much, darling. For one thing the piano's out
of tune. And so am I. (*Looks at him from above, sadly.*) You
come and sit here then.

*Takes him by the hand, leads him to the chair nearest the
piano, then goes to the piano, begins to play uncertainly.
The piano is out of tune.*
MOLLY *makes a face. After a moment she begins to sing,
very loudly, but nicely, 'And did those feet'.*
EVE *enters from the back, stands listening.*
TEDDY *is evidently straining to hear, his foot beating out of
time to the music.*

TEDDY (*as* MOLLY *is fading out*). There. There Evie. She wrote
it herself. What do you think of it?

EVE. I think it's lovely.

MOLLY. Why Evie, you're tone deaf!

EVE. Perhaps I am. But I know a nice voice when I hear one.
Dinner's ready.

MOLLY *comes over, takes* TEDDY's *hand; they go through
back, and as* EVE *closes the door behind them; Lights.*

Scene Two

*A week or so later. Mid-afternoon. The room is full of sunlight,
the conservatory door is open.*
   OLIVER *enters through the conservatory, furtively. He is
wearing an open-necked shirt, baggy gardening trousers. He
looks towards the kitchen, back, then towards the door, left,
then goes to the sofa, on which is* MOLLY's *handbag. Opens the
handbag, takes out a package of cigarettes and the lighter. Quickly
extracts a cigarette, puts it in his pocket, then another, which he
lights. Puts the lighter back in the handbag, closes it. Stands
smoking, looking around.*
   EVE *enters from the back. Stands watching* OLIVER.
   OLIVER, *suddenly conscious of another presence, turns.
They stare at each other.*

OLIVER. I've finished digging up them weeds around the garage,
Missus.

EVE. And have you done the hedge?

OLIVER. No, Missus, I — I don't know where the shears is.

EVE. We don't keep them in the sitting-room, Oliver. Perhaps they're under the potato sacking on the second shelf in the conservatory where I told you to put them the last time you used them, have you looked?

OLIVER. No Missus.

EVE. Have you put the weeds in the compost?

OLIVER. No Miss.

EVE. Then do that first. Then the hedge. And oh, Oliver — (EVE *gets an ashtray, comes towards* OLIVER, *holds it out.*) In here, please.

OLIVER *stubs out the cigarette.*

EVE. Now here are two things for you to understand, Oliver. Firstly, we don't like you wandering into the house whenever you feel like it, and secondly we don't like you smoking in the house, you left a saucer full of stubs in my kitchen after your lunch today. All right?

OLIVER. Yes Missus. (*Sulkily.*)

EVE. And by the way, I'm not Missus, I'm Miss. Miss Mace. (*Attempts a more friendly tone. Little pause.*) Is anything the matter?

OLIVER. Well, Missus — Miss. The only thing — well, I mean, I was told it was going to be fixing the Alvis and driving it mainly, that was my work, and there was a bit of gardening on the side, but I mean I've got the Alvis fixed, but I've only got to drive it twice in two weeks, it's been gardening all the time, and even painting the inside of the garage.

EVE. I see. Well, Oliver, If you're not satisfied with the conditions of your employment, you're quite at liberty to leave. Is that what you want to do?

OLIVER. No Missus.

EVE. Miss.

OLIVER. No Miss.

EVE. I'm sure you don't. So you'd better get on with it, hadn't you?

OLIVER (*after a pause*). Yes, Miss. (*Turns to go.*)

EVE (*looks into the ashtray*). Oliver. What cigarettes do you smoke?

OLIVER. Any sort, Missus. Miss.

EVE. Including the sort that Mrs Treadley smokes?

OLIVER (*shrugs*). I don't know what sort she smokes.

EVE. She smokes this sort. (*Holding up stub.*) Did you take one of hers?

OLIVER. No Miss!

EVE. I think you did, Oliver. That's what you were doing in here, wasn't it?

OLIVER. No Miss, I never!

EVE. Please don't lie, Oliver.

OLIVER (*as* MOLLY *enters*). I'm not lying, Miss!

MOLLY (*looking from one to the other*). What's going on, it sounds thrilling!

EVE. I'm just trying to find out whether Oliver's been helping himself to your cigarettes.

OLIVER. I didn't, Miss.

MOLLY. Oh, I do hope you didn't, Oliver, I'm terribly low and I do hate to be caught without one. Shall I check and see how I'm off? (*Goes over to handbag, opens it, looks into the cigarette package.*) About a dozen, I suppose that'll do, could you remember some, Evie, if you're going shopping. (*Little pause.*) Are you doing something in the garden, Oliver?

OLIVER. I've got to put weeds in the compost and then clip the hedge, Miss.

MOLLY. Such a nice day for being outside.

OLIVER. Yes, Miss. (*Smirks at* EVE, *goes out.*)

EVE. Molly, I know he helped himself.

MOLLY (*lighting a cigarette*). Yes, darling, I expect you're right.

EVE. Well, if there's one thing I hate it's a pilferer. And a liar.

MOLLY. Well we all have our pet aversions, I detest ghastly scenes and boys getting shrill all over something extremely trivial, darling.

EVE. I see. (*Turns, goes out, back.*)

MOLLY. I see. I see. Pretty please with sugar on it. (*Imitating first* EVE, *then herself*.) Oh God — (*She gets up.*) Evie! (*Makes to go back.*)

TEDDY (*enters, left*). Hey Moll, you nearly let me fall asleep again, you ready?

MOLLY. What? What for darling?

TEDDY. Our walk.

MOLLY. What walk?

TEDDY. Aren't you coming for a walk?

MOLLY. But darling, we worked it all out at lunch, now we've got the piano tuned at last I was going to try and settle to some song writing, and you were going to go for a walk.

TEDDY. We're going to Gwyllup, it's five miles.

MOLLY. No darling, we were going to *drive* to Gwyllup another day —

TEDDY. No, no, walk.

MOLLY. Anyway, not this afternoon —

TEDDY. You're smoking again.

MOLLY. So I am, I am.

TEDDY. If you don't want to, you'd better not.

MOLLY. But I do. I do.

TEDDY. Then we'd better get started.

MOLLY. No, I mean smoke — (*Stubs the cigarette out irritably.*)

REDDY. Do you or don't you, I can't make it out.

EVE (*enters back*). I'm just going to do the shopping.

TEDDY. What?

EVE. I've got down tomatoes, oranges, cauliflower, the beef to be collected, four skewers —

MOLLY. Oh darling, do come in properly, it can't be any good for your throat — baying at me from over there.

TEDDY. I'm going to walk to Gwyllup. The question is whether you are.

EVE. I'm sorry. I didn't mean to bay at you. (*Frostily.*)

TEDDY. I can perfectly well go by myself.

EVE. I just wanted to know if you wanted to add anything.

MOLLY. Add anything? To the skewers and the four cauliflowers?

EVE. To the shopping list.

TEDDY. When you two have sorted it out, whatever it is that's so
important to you, I'll be upstairs in my room. I don't want to
keep interrupting you ladies when you're nattering about
something important — (*Going out, slams the door, left.*)

There is a pause.

MOLLY. Omigod! We go to all the trouble of getting that little
man over from Guildford so that I can play the piano properly
at last, and perhaps even, who knows? compose a song, and
when I actually at last arrange to spend an afternoon at the
piano, I find myself harassed with tales about youths stealing
cigarettes, and grown men demanding to be taken for walks —
it's too much, it's too, too much! (*Takes out a cigarette,
lights it.*)

EVE *turns away, her face working.*

MOLLY (*looks at* EVE, *looks away angrily, draws on her cigarette*).
Sorry darling. Didn't mean to be ratty. Forgive please. (*Little
pause.*) Pretty please, with sugar on it.

EVE. I expect it *is* all my fault. *I'm* sorry, Molly. The truth is,
I've got a bit of a headache, this weather's a little close for
me. (*Attempts a little laugh.*) That always means it's going to
rain. Sorry Moll.

MOLLY. Oh poor darling, can I get you an aspirin?

EVE. No — nothing does any good until it rains.

MOLLY. Anyway, you mustn't think of going to the shops — why
don't you have a nice lie-down?

EVE. Oh, I'll be all right. Really. I shouldn't have made such a
fuss over Oliver.

MOLLY. Someone's got to make fusses for us, darling, and as
you're the only grown-up in the house, it'd better be you. We
are childish, aren't we, Teddy and I?

EVE. Of course you're not.

MOLLY. Yes we are.

EVE. Well — I've always liked children.

MOLLY. Really, darling? I wouldn't have thought you'd much to do with them before.

EVE. Oh yes. I helped to look after some once. A long time ago.

MOLLY. Did you? (*Abruptly.*) I'd like a child. Do you think it's too late for me?

Little pause. EVE *looks embarrassed.*

MOLLY. I mean adopt one of course. Now that I'm back in England — home again. One could easily adopt one, couldn't one? What do you think?

EVE. I think it's the most marvellous idea!

MOLLY. After all, if we keep this place on, we've lots of room. He could have the small room as a bedroom, and the room opposite as a play-room and I could move across the hall to be next to him — and even if we don't stay here we could find somewhere else just as big — you see how I've been working it out?

EVE. Oh Moll!

MOLLY. And you wouldn't run away if we did?

EVE. I'd love it! And what does Teddy think?

MOLLY. Oh, I haven't mentioned it to him yet. One thing at a time for the poor darling — first England, then a child, then if we get on with that one perhaps another to go with it and so on, we may end up with a flock of them — (*laughing*) — we'd have to keep some out in the fields!

EVE.(*laughs*). Oh Moll!

TEDDY (*enters left*). I'm not going to doze through the afternoon, have you two fixed it all up between yourselves, yet?

MOLLY. Oh yes, darling, completely. Haven't we, Evie?

EVE (*smiling*). Yes.

TEDDY. Then you're ready to hike to Gwyllup? Or do I go on my own?

MOLLY. Oh darling, do you mind if I try out the lovely piano you've had fixed up for me? Do you?

TEDDY. You're saying no?

MOLLY. Darling, I will, if you like.

TEDDY. I'm going anyway, as that's what we arranged.

MOLLY. Besides, Evie says it's going to rain, and you know how
    bad that can be for your ears — why don't you take a little
    local stroll.

TEDDY. I'm going to Gwyllup. (*Pause.*) I'm going to Gwyllup.

MOLLY (*hesitates*). Then at least take your raincoat and your
    mackintosh hat.

TEDDY. What?

MOLLY. Your raincoat and mackintosh hat.

TEDDY. What for? It's not going to rain. 'Bye. (*Stamps out
    through the conservatory.*)

MOLLY. Oh damn, damn, what shall I do, if it rains into his ears
    — and he *will* go to Gwyllup too, he's so stubborn — and if I
    go after him now he'll just stump angrily along —

EVE (*getting up*). I'll take them to him. (*Runs to door, left,
    returns at once with hat and coat.*)

MOLLY. Oh thank you darling. But really somebody ought to go
    with him, I know it's a lot to ask — will you?

EVE (*hesitates, then smiles*). Of course Moll.

MOLLY. You are a darling — and they say Gwyllup's very
    beautiful.

EVE (*runs through the conservatory, with hat and coat. As she
    does so, she calls*). Oliver — Oliver — run after Mr Treadley, tell
    him to wait a minute, hurry, hurry!

MOLLY *stands listening for a moment, then goes into the
conservatory, stands watching, still visible to the audience, then
returns. Goes to the cigarettes, picks one out, lights it, puffs
on it. Sits down to smoke. After a moment gets up, stands
uncertainly, kicks off her shoes, then wanders over to the
piano, picks out a tune, tries to play, then crashes a discord,
sits puffing on her cigarette. Gets up, paces about restlessly,
then goes to the cocktail cabinet, pours herself a gin, walks
determinedly back to the piano, sits down, gets up, goes over,
lights another cigarette, sits down with the drink.*

MOLLY. Alone at last. (*Pause, then in a desolate voice.*) Omigod!
    (*Pause, suddenly shakes her head from side to side, stops,
    puts her fingers to her forehead.*) Omigod! (*Collapses back
    into the sofa.*)

ER. Yes. She worked in a tea shop.

LY (*drinks again*). And is that all you did with her?

ER. We went to the films sometimes.

LY. Were you lovers?

ER. What?

LY. Lovers.

ere is a pause.

LY. Here — (*pours a drink of gin, brings it to* OLIVER) have
ip of this.

ER. What is it?

LY. A truth drink. To help you tell me whether you were
ers. It's all right, I swear I won't tell your Dad if you
omise not to tell mine. Husband. Sip and tell, Oliver.

ER (*sips*). Well — (*Sips again.*) No Miss.

LY. No, won't tell, or no, weren't lovers?

ER. Weren't — um, lovers.

LY. Oh dear, oh dear, why not?

ER (*laughs embarrassed.*) Don't know anything about any
that.

LY. Any of what? (*Goes over to him, takes the shears off
lap, puts them on the floor.*) There. Any of what?

ER. My Dad wouldn't stand for any of that. He'd kill me
I did anything like that.

LY (*standing close to him*). Then what happened between
urself and this girl, what was her name?

ER. Rosie. Rosie Hitchens. Well — just one day she turned
ound when I went over and said her Mum didn't want her to
me any more.

LY. And she didn't?

ER (*after a pause*). No.

LY (*after a pause*). Poor Oliver. Poor Rosie Hutchings, come
that.

ER. Hitchens. Her name was.

LY. Is your mother dead?

OLIVER *appears in the conservatory. He is carrying the coat
and the mackintosh hat.* MOLLY *doesn't notice him.* OLIVER
clears his throat.

MOLLY (*looks at him*). Oh hello. He sent them back, did he?

OLIVER. Yes Miss. He said to say he doesn't need them. And he
says thank you, um, for —

MOLLY. What?

OLIVER. Well, Evie, Miss.

MOLLY (*smiles wryly*). Thank you. Well, sling them — sling
them over there somewhere, would you?

OLIVER *puts them on the end of the sofa.*

MOLLY. And how's everything in the garden?

OLIVER. I got the weeds on the compost, I'm going to start on
the hedge.

MOLLY. How lucky — to have something you've got to do.

OLIVER. Yes Miss.

Slight pause. OLIVER *goes into the conservatory, clatters
about, just in sight.* MOLLY *looks towards the conservatory,
watches.*

OLIVER. Just getting the shears, Miss. (*Holds them up.*)

MOLLY. Come in for a moment, Oliver, please. (*With authority.*)

OLIVER *enters, carrying the shears.*

MOLLY. Two, Oliver.

OLIVER. Miss?

MOLLY (*holds up two fingers*). You took two of my cigarettes,
Oliver.

OLIVER. I didn't! Miss, I swear —

MOLLY. Oh Oliver, don't, please. It makes you sound like a
goose when you protest — you honk.

OLIVER. But — (*Stops.*)

MOLLY (*gets cigarettes, holds package out to* OLIVER). Here,
have another one.

OLIVER. No thank you, Miss.

MOLLY. Oh go on. You mustn't mind my knowing about you

being a liar, I lie all the time, all the time, about lots of things, about cigarettes too. I promise I won't smoke more than five a day, my husband thinks it's bad for my health, but of course I sneak extra ones, like now with you, he'd have a fit if he could see me puffing away. Do you know what he'd do? He'd put me across his knee and spank me, Oliver. Yes, he would. What do you think of that?

OLIVER. Well Miss – (*Gives a strange half laugh.*)

MOLLY. Now I've told you all that, you've got to take one, haven't you?

OLIVER *hesitates, then takes one.*

MOLLY. I bet your Dad doesn't put you across his knee and spank you, at least not any more, does he?

OLIVER. No Miss. (*Laughs again.*)

MOLLY. You did take them, didn't you?

OLIVER. Yes Miss.

MOLLY. There, now we've both confessed. But I'm very sorry Oliver, now I shall have to punish you. You do realise that, you can't pinch my cigarettes and then lie and bluster about it and not expect punishment, can you? (*She allows a long pause.*) Sit down please, Oliver.

OLIVER, *after a moment, sits.*

MOLLY. Do you know what I'm going to do to you?

OLIVER *shakes his head.*

MOLLY. I'm going to teach you a lesson, Oliver. I'm going to make you sit here and talk to me. (*Laughs.*) Just for a little, do you mind?

OLIVER (*smiles*). No Miss. Except there's the hedge and she goes on at me.

MOLLY. Oh, *her*! Don't worry about her, Oliver, I'll protect you from her! (*Pause.*) Tell me, do you think it's going to rain?

OLIVER. Yes Miss.

MOLLY. Oh don't say that, why?

OLIVER. Because it feels like rain. And my Dad said it would.

MOLLY. And is your Dad always right?

OLIVER. Usually Miss.

MOLLY. About everything, or just about the wea

OLIVER. Well, about the weather, anyway, Miss.

MOLLY. How does he know, by sniffing the air, finger up or rising at six for shepherds' warnin

OLIVER. No Miss.

MOLLY. How then?

OLIVER. He listen to the radio Miss, at breakfast. *a pause.*)

MOLLY. Well, clever old Dad. (*Laughing.*) I bet y lie to him.

OLIVER. Oh no Miss.

MOLLY. What about?

OLIVER. Miss?

MOLLY. What do you lie to him about?

OLIVER. I said I didn't, Miss.

MOLLY. Yes that was a lie to me. What do you lie Come on, Oliver, do tell me. Please, pretty pleas know you do.

OLIVER. How, Miss?

MOLLY. Because if we didn't lie to people we love we wouldn't be able to love and live with them. S

Gets up, goes to cocktail cabinet, pours herself a OLIVER.

OLIVER (*after a pause*). Well, only about Guildford over at Guildford. That's all.

MOLLY. And what *do* you do over at Guildford?

During this scene, and by imperceptible degrees, t darkens to suggest the sky darkening.

MOLLY. Oh of course, you've got a girl there. (*Drink*

OLIVER. Well – (*Shrugs.*)

MOLLY. Haven't you?

OLVERI. Not any more. There was a girl. I used to ha her sometimes.

MOLLY. Only tea?

OLIVER. Yes Miss. When I was born.

MOLLY. You're terribly fond of your Dad, aren't you? Tell me, what do you do together? I mean in the evenings, or the weekends?

OLIVER. Well — we go shooting.

MOLLY. Do you, oh, dear, what do you shoot?

OLIVER. Only rabbits.

MOLLY. *Only* rabbits? Oh Oliver. And do you kill many of them?

OLIVER. Quite a few. My Dad's a good shot. I'm not bad.

MOLLY. What do you think, when you see them dead?

OLIVER. That they're dead, Miss. Dead rabbits. For pie.

MOLLY. Have you got a dog?

OLIVER. We had one once, Miss.

MOLLY. What happened to it?

OLIVER. It got run over.

MOLLY. And what did you think, when you saw it dead.

OLIVER. It was in the middle of the Guildford road, where all the lorries run. My Dad took me down to see it, lying there squashed, I was only six about.

MOLLY. Why did he do that?

OLIVER. To show me what happened if I was careless on the road.

MOLLY. Omigod, Oliver! And what did you say, when you saw it there?

OLIVER. I said (*thinks*) were we going to have it for lunch.

MOLLY. You didn't!

OLIVER. No Miss. We had it for supper.

MOLLY (*after a moment, laughing*). You're making fun of me! That's nice. (*Pours more gin into* OLIVER's *glass.*) There! You see how it helps. And me. (*Pours some into her own.*) Because now I'm going to tell you why I hate to think of shooting only rabbits even, and you mustn't laugh at me, promise?

OLIVER. Miss.

MOLLY. You see, I hate anything being killed by people. Ever since I heard about something very dreadful — about how

these great Canadian men with their red necks and tartan caps
on their heads drive down to the beach in their trucks and
they catch the seals, the mother seals and the baby seals, and
they beat their heads in with clubs and hammers. (*Sits down
beside him.*) Yes they do, Oliver, and sometimes the mothers
stay a little way out in the sea, watching, while these — these
men! — skin their babies while they're still alive often, skin
them for their furs. Dreadful. Dreadful. They have such big
eyes and they stare at their babies — D'you see, Oliver. (*Looks
at him intently.*) I wrote a song about it. It was broadcast on
the radio over there, and played right across Nova Scotia. But
it didn't stop them. That's when I knew I couldn't live in
Canada any more, amongst people like that. So don't shoot
any rabbits ever again. Please don't, Oliver. Pretty please.
With sugar on it. (*There is a pause.*) Oh I know, you've got to,
for your Dad's sake. You'll just have to try to miss them, that's
all. For my sake. Aim — (*raises her arm at* OLIVER, *jerks at
the last second*) sideways. (*Laughs.*) But don't hit your Dad.
For his sake. Are you happy with us?

OLIVER. Oh yes, Miss.

MOLLY. I watch you sometimes, Oliver. Did you know that?
When you're in the garden. As busy as bees. Mowing the lawn
yesterday. I watched you from an upstairs window. And then
on your knees weeding this morning. But I haven't seen you
recite poetry to the flowers. No. And sometimes you even look
a trifle — sulky. There. I've said it. As if you weren't truly and
really deeply happy with us. Why not, Oliver?

OLIVER. I am, Miss. (*Pause.*) Well.

MOLLY. No, go on. On.

OLIVER. She gets at me a lot, Miss.

MOLLY. Oh, she gets at us all a lot, pay her no mind, we don't.
When she gets at me I pay her out my very best smile and say
forgive me, Evie, pretty please, with sugar on it. You can try
that. Because then you can ignore her and be rude to her or
whatever you want. What else is wrong?

OLIVER. Nothing, Miss. Well.

MOLLY. Oh, Oliver. On.

OLIVER. Well, only about the car, that's all. I mean I was taken
on to do the car, but now I've got it fixed up I've only taken it
out twice, the rest of it's been gardening and painting the

garage, and the other day it was sash cords even she made me do.

MOLLY. I'm so glad you've told me this, Oliver. I'll have a word with Teddy when he gets back. (*Pours herself another drink.*) I promise you more outings in the car. I never break my promises you know.

OLIVER. Oh, I don't really mind. It's just that that's what I thought I was being taken on to do mainly and, well, they make jokes about it at Sprinkley's and up at the pub, because my Dad told them all I was going to be a chauffeur and they say if you're a chauffeur where's your uniform. My Dad doesn't like that.

MOLLY. If your Dad doesn't like it, that settles it. Although I don't know about a uniform — I don't know if I'd like you so much in a uniform. Will you teach me to drive. Oliver, and keep it a secret from my Dad. Will you?

OLIVER. Yes Miss.

MOLLY. And then when you've taught me I'll show him I can. Eh? Oliver? (*Laughs.*) If you promise to teach me then you shall have a uniform — even though I like you just as you are, Oliver. I like you very much. You do know that, don't you?

(*They stare at each other*)

MOLLY. Do you like him?

OLIVER. Who?

MOLLY. Teddy.

OLIVER. Yes, Miss.

MOLLY. So do I. Even though he calls you boy and Ollie and Oliver Treefsir?

OLIVER. Oh, I don't mind that. It's just his way.

MOLLY. Because he's deaf, you see. It's so sad. Because people when they're deaf can't have normal friendly conversations with each other, as we're having, so they have to find little tricks of their own to show normal friendliness, and to hide their deafness too. And he's very friendly. More than normally.

OLIVER. He doesn't really —

MOLLY. What?

OLIVER (*hesitates*). Put you over his knee, does he?

MOLLY (*stares at* OLIVER). D'you mind?

OLIVER. Miss. (*Laughs.*) He doesn't! Does he?

MOLLY. I'm so worried, Oliver, about his getting his ears wet.
And your saying it's going to rain — (*Goes over to the
window, looks out.*) It's darker, getting darker. It *is* raining
a little. Oh damn! Oh, poor Teddy. But it's delicious, too, isn't
it, the two of us snug inside, talking and drinking, while
outside — (*shivers*) delicious. (*Takes a gulp of gin.*) Do you like
me, Oliver?

OLIVER. Miss?

MOLLY. Or do you think I'm just a silly old vamp, do you?

OLIVER. No, Miss.

MOLLY. What then? Say it. You must say it. I said it to you.

OLIVER. Like you, Miss.

MOLLY. But I don't frighten you, do I?

OLIVER. No Miss.

MOLLY. We'll have another cigarette, shall we?

> *Goes with cigarettes, offers one to* OLIVER, *lights it for
> him. She is staring at him. Takes a step around the side of the
> sofa, puts her foot on the shears, stumbles, cries out.*

OLIVER (*gets to his feet*). What is it, Miss, what is it?

MOLLY. I've cut myself — my foot — (*Tries to see the sole of her
foot.*) Can you see?

> OLIVER, *bending some yards away, stares.*

MOLLY. Look properly — take it — (*Stretches out her leg.*)

OLIVER (*takes her foot gingerly*). I can't see any cut, Miss.

MOLLY. But it's wet — I can feel the bleeding —

OLIVER. No Miss — that's your drink — I can smell it — that's
all —

MOLLY. But it hurts, oh God, it hurts — (*Loses balance, hops.*)

OLIVER. Miss — Miss — (*Lets go of* MOLLY's *leg.*)

> MOLLY *stumbles towards* OLIVER, *who puts out his arms to
> catch her.*

MOLLY. Oh Oliver — (*clinging to him*) it did hurt — it did —

OLIVER. Miss. (*In alarm.*)

MOLLY. Oliver — don't be frightened. Don't be.

OLIVER. Miss?

> MOLLY *begins to kiss* OLIVER, *ravenously.* OLIVER
> *clumsily responds. Lights down to sound of rain. Rain
> continues through the darkness.*

Scene Three

*About an hour later. Lights up to greyness. Still raining heavily.
OLIVER is sitting on the sofa, putting on his socks. He has already
put on his underpants. The raincoat is spread under him, across
the sofa, the waterproof side up, there are cushions on the floor.
MOLLY is in her underpants, doing up her bra. She is standing
some way from OLIVER. She is dressing quickly.
OLIVER stops dressing, watches MOLLY. His face works. He
turns, rolls into the sofa, puts his arm over his face.*

MOLLY (*not noticing*). Oh that rain, that bloody rain — but
they'll have found somewhere in the village — or a tree — the
poor man — next time I'll check the weather with your Dad or
the wireless — (*Dressing through this, turns, looks at* OLIVER.)
Oliver — (*Goes over to him.*) Oliver, darling, what is it? (*Sits
down on the sofa next to him, tries to remove* OLIVER's *arm
from his face.*) Oliver — don't — you mustn't — here, here —
(*Pulls his arm away.*) Why are you? Is it because you're unhappy?
Are you unhappy?

OLIVER (*shakes his head*). No, Miss.

MOLLY. Because you're happy then?

> OLIVER, *crying, turns his face away.*

MOLLY (*taking his face in her hands*). Because you're happy?

OLIVER. Miss. I don't know Miss.

MOLLY (*cuddles him*). There Oliver, nothing to cry for, nothing
to cry for. I'm glad, I am, yes I am, and I want you to be
happy, but you mustn't cry —

OLIVER (*embraces her with sudden and desperate passion*).
Please Miss please Miss please Miss —

MOLLY. What darling? What?

OLIVER. You won't send me away Miss.

MOLLY. No, no — of course not — just for now — just for a little
while — but there'll be other times. I promise you. Lots of
other times, but we mustn't let them find out, must we? They
wouldn't understand, and I wouldn't want to hurt Teddy, he
loves me, you know, and I must care for him too, mustn't I,
and not let him be hurt, so now I've got to put everything
right and you must finish getting dressed, darling, and help me
by being as quick as you can, darling, before they come back —
do you understand, darling? Do you?

OLIVER *nods.*

MOLLY. Go on then. Go on, my darling — (*Gets up, finishes
dressing.*)

OLIVER *goes on dressing, sniffing.*

MOLLY (*comes over, buttons his shirt*). Now you go now, my
darling — (*leads him to the door left*) there's a good boy —
(*Kisses him.*)

OLIVER *goes out left, there is a pause. He comes back, rushes
over to* MOLLY, *throws his arms around her.*

MOLLY (*strokes his head*). I'll see you soon. I promise. And I
never break my promises.

They separate. OLIVER *stands looking at* MOLLY.

MOLLY. Go, Oliver. (*Gently, leads him out left and sounds of her
saying goodbye quickly at the front door. Front door closes,
off,* MOLLY *enters left as* TEDDY, *followed by* EVE, *enters
the conservatory, right.*

TEDDY *is soaking, mud-stained. Followed by* EVE, *also
soaking.*

MOLLY (*stares, shocked*). Omigod — darling, what happened?

TEDDY. Well, here I am, Moll, back from a stroll in your nice
quiet countryside, right in the middle of the fields, eh Evie,
then wham, right from out of your nice quiet clouds, wham,
wham, wham! (*Laughs.*)

MOLLY. Darling, you must get into some dry clothes. (*Getting up,
going to him.*)

EVE. And a hot bath!

TEDDY *has gone to cocktail cabinet, pours himself an enormous Scotch.*

TEDDY. And there we were, Evie and me, (*gulping the Scotch*) licking across the field in the dark, sheets of it coming down, and there was this tree Evie saw, on a bank and a ditch running under it, anyway wouldn't pass in Novia Scotia for a river (*laughs*) and I swayed on the edge, eh, Evie?

MOLLY. Darling, tell me afterwards, get changed now!

TEDDY. Felt like minutes, rocking and swaying, and Evie had hold of my arm pulling me back, but a hand shot out of nowhere and down I went.

MOLLY. A hand?

TEDDY. And down I went, right Evie?

MOLLY. You were pushed?

TEDDY. And down I went, right, Evie, Evie almost coming with me. (*Laughs.*) So don't you two talk to me about your friendly English countryside again, we've got bob-cat, bear and skunk in Nova Scotia but we don't have anything you can't see or hear or understand come up behind you and tumble you into the mud for no damn reason — (*gulps again*) raining inside my skull — (*pulls out the hearing aid*) damn thing, damned thing, battery soaking — get it fixed, fixed tomorrow — (*Takes another gulp, stands staring at* MOLLY.) Hey, Moll!

MOLLY. He's trembling — darling! He's feverish — come on, darling, we must get you to a bath and bed — come along. (*Pulls* TEDDY *towards the door.*)

TEDDY. I'm all right — I'm all right — (*Goes out.*)

MOLLY (*before she closes the door, turns, stares at* EVE). I told you to make him take his raincoat and his mackintosh hat! I *told* you! (*Goes out.*)

EVE *stands for a moment. Then bends, automatically. Picks up* TEDDY's *hat.*)

EVE (*in an emotional voice*). It's jolly well not fair! (*Suddenly takes in the chaos of the room, glasses, cushions, etc.*)

Lights.

CURTAIN.

Act Two

Scene One

A week or so later. The sun is shining. It is mid-afternoon. EVE is sitting with some knitting on her lap. She is staring ahead. There is the sound of a door closing, off, up left. Then quick footsteps, EVE starts knitting.

MOLLY. Hello darling, seen my handbag?

EVE. On the sofa.

MOLLY. You are clever. (*Going to the handbag.*)

EVE. You usually leave it on the sofa. Have you got Teddy's drops?

MOLLY. Oh yes, here they are. (*Fishes them out of the handbag, puts them on the table.*)

EVE. He always needs them first thing, when he wakes.

MOLLY. I know, poor darling. Isn't that growing — Teddy'll be so thrilled. I wish I could knit.

EVE. Do you? It's not difficult.

MOLLY. No, I suppose it can't be, as so many dolts can. It's one of those activities I always thought I'd find myself doing when I grew up — like putting on grey hair and wrinkles.

EVE. Indeed?

MOLLY. Oh darling, I didn't mean — (*Laughs.*)

EVE (*smiles coldly*). Are you going out?

MOLLY. Yes, I've got an appointment with Oliver for a driving lesson. What about you?

EVE. Oh no. I don't think Teddy should be left alone at the moment.

MOLLY. But darling, he's asleep, I've just checked.

EVE. Yesterday when you were having a driving lesson and I was down here he woke up and thought he was alone in the house. He was quite fretful for a good half hour.

MOLLY. I must say, darling, that doesn't sound like a good half hour. (*Hesitates.*) In that case why don't you go out and I'll stay in, it's your turn.

EVE. No. I'd as soon get on with this. Besides Oliver will be expecting you.

MOLLY. Oh, I can always find something else for him to do.

EVE. I'm glad he's settling down so well. Since you moved him into the house.

MOLLY. Hasn't he been a Godsend.

EVE. Yes. Mrs Shepherd says he's funny in the head. She came around yesterday morning. She'd heard he was living in so she came around especially to warn us. She said he was funny in the head. That's why they dismissed him. Her husband caught him in their bedroom, going through her underwear drawer.

MOLLY. Oh, don't you worry, darling. Your underwear drawer is quite safe. Oliver's told me all about it.

EVE. I see. You don't think it peculiar even then?

MOLLY. Nothing like as peculiar as Mrs Shepherd, trekking all the way up here to tell us about it.

EVE. Oh well, as long as *you* don't mind —

MOLLY. No, I don't mind, darling. Not at all. And if you're not keen to go out I'll get some fresh air. (*Gets up, goes towards the conservatory.*)

EVE (*watches her, and as* MOLLY *gets to the conservatory door*). Oh by the way, Molly, as soon as Teddy's better I shall be leaving. (*Little pause.*) I thought I should tell you now, so you'd have time to find someone more suitable.

MOLLY (*takes out a cigarette, lights it*). More suitable to what, darling?

EVE. To what's going on in this house.

MOLLY. What *is* going on in this house?

EVE. Wasn't Oliver in your room last night?

MOLLY. Yes, he did look in to say goodnight and to ask how Teddy was.

EVE. He stayed the whole night.

MOLLY *makes to exclaim.*

EVE. Please don't lie to me, Moll, I couldn't bear it. I heard Teddy stumbling down the hall at midnight. It was only by the grace of God that I managed to stop him opening the door on the two of you. He'd had a nightmare, and wanted comforting. Thank God *he* couldn't hear what I heard.

There is a honk from outside, right.

MOLLY. Omigod! Thank you, Evie!

EVE. Oh it wasn't you I was thinking of, it was Teddy.

MOLLY. I know. Thank you. Teddy and I don't sleep together, surely you've realised that.

EVE. But — but he's still your husband. You married him.

MOLLY. Yes. And I do my best to make him happy, haven't you noticed? I get drunk with him, and cuddle him, and let him slap me on the bottom — all — all that. It's enough for Teddy. It's not always enough for me.

EVE. You mean — you've done this before?

MOLLY. From time to time. Though not as often as I want to.

EVE. Oh, you sound so hard — so hard.

MOLLY. Do I, darling? Sorry. You've been companion-housekeeper to a wicked woman, darling, you see. I need my sex. There. I've said it.

EVE. Then you had no right to marry Teddy.

MOLLY. Hadn't I? He wanted me to.

EVE. But what did you marry him for? His money?

MOLLY. I admit I wouldn't have if he'd been an impoverished — (*Gestures.*)

EVE. Garage hand. Like Oliver Treefe, you mean?

MOLLY. Well, unlike Oliver, Teddy would have been a sixty-year-old impoverished garage hand when I married him, so I probably wouldn't have married him, no.

EVE. I don't understand.

MOLLY. What, darling? What don't you understand?

EVE. You who could have married anybody —

MOLLY. Not when I married Teddy. Don't forget he *was* sixty, and I was *all* of thirty — and he was quite a dynamic Halifax businessman and I was one of those, you know, glamorous English divorcees that end up in countries like Canada on spec.

EVE. I didn't know you'd been married before.

MOLLY. Gets worse and worse, doesn't it, darling. Yes. Married before. Sorry. There were no children though, other than the two of us. Then he began to grow up, and left me for someone who would look after him properly. I've never been very good at getting meals on tables and organising homes and curtains and housekeeping — all the things you're so good at doing. He's a solicitor in Harrow now, I think it is, with no doubt children and all the rest of the things — (*gestures*) he couldn't imagine me providing him with. (*Pause.*) Actually, I did almost manage a child, but it miscarried. He blamed me for that — my fecklessness — because we'd been to a party and I drank a mite too much and slipped and fell down the stairs. He rather hated me — (*Pause.*) So after I'd set him free I took a plunge, and went off to Canada, where I just managed to keep my head above water doing lady-like little jobs and being glamorous and English — all the right things to be if one wanted one of those ghastly Canadian men as a lover, you know, balding and fattening, but no good for husbands, because they were already. Until Teddy came along. I was working as a part-time receptionist sort of person who did a little piano playing and drinking in the hotel and he was the first eligible male I've infatuated. Except there is just this little thing wrong with him, I don't know what, but he doesn't have sex, I don't believe he ever has. But apart from that and already beginning to deafen he was quite dynamic and infatuated. There. Now do you understand, Evie?

EVE. I suppose I might, oh I wouldn't approve but I might understand if it were some — some man you'd — you'd — but Oliver Treefe! Can't you see what he is?

MOLLY. What is he, darling? Other than peculiar in the head?

EVE. Well, for one thing he's — he's twenty years younger than you.

MOLLY. Is that worse than being almost thirty years older?

EVE. But he's — he's completely uneducated. He's not even
particularly nice to look at. Even I can see that. He's a
common, loutish —

MOLLY. Stop it, Eve. Please. The truth is, Ollie and I —

EVE. Ollie and you! Ollie and you! No, I can't stop it, I jolly well
think it's disgusting. Disgusting!

MOLLY (*in a sudden scream*). We're all disgusting!

There is a pause.

EVE (*gets up*). Well *I'm* not, Molly Treadley. No, *I'm* not!

OLIVER *enters through the conservatory. He is wearing a
chauffeur's uniform, carrying a gap and gauntlets.*

OLIVER. Oh, excuse me, Miss, I've been honking for you outside.

MOLLY. Honking for me?

EVE *exits, left.*

OLIVER. She in one of her bad moods?

MOLLY. A touch edgy, perhaps. (*Little pause.*) Look darling,
I'm sorry, but I'd better not come this afternoon, after all.

OLIVER. Why not?

MOLLY. Why don't you give your Dad that ride you've been
promising him. He's scarcely seen you this last ten days.

OLIVER. He's working.

MOLLY. Well darling, anything you want to do — do. (*Smiles at
him.*)

OLIVER. I want to go out with you. You promised me, Moll. To
make up for all that hanging about outside Gracey's this
morning.

MOLLY. I know darling, I'm sorry, but really I can't.

OLIVER. It *is* because of her, isn't it?

MOLLY. I suppose so. Because of her and him and you and me —
it's all very complicated and I'm not up to explaining it and
you wouldn't like it if I did, darling, but what it comes
down to is that it would make everything worse if we skipped
off right now.

OLIVER. It's not fair. I've been sitting out there, honking and

waiting and honking and waiting and I've changed the oil even,
and now you tell me you can't come out and won't tell me
why, but it's because of her and him — I know it is.

MOLLY. Oliver!

OLIVER *makes to say something else.*

MOLLY. No, don't say another word Ollie. Not now. Just go.
For your sake, darling.

OLIVER (*looks at her, turns, makes as if to exit through the
conservatory, stops*). It's true what they say, isn't it? That you
hooked him for his money and car and that. That's what
Sprinkley said from the beginning, the first time he saw you,
and my Dad's said something about you and him, he thinks
it's wrong, and Bob Howells making jokes in the pub, if he
pays you for every go or how many times a week you have to
let him do it, they were all laughing at his jokes in the pub
about him and you. All of them. That's what I have to sit and
listen to.

MOLLY (*goes to* OLIVER).Who is Bob Howells, darling?

OLIVER. He's Sprinkley's cousin, he —

MOLLY *slaps* OLIVER *across the face.*
OLIVER *stands for a moment, then runs over to the sofa, falls
onto it.*

MOLLY (*looks at him, goes over to him*). If you ever — ever —
talk to me like that again, it's back to Bob Howells and
Sprinkley's for you, my boy.

OLIVER. You wouldn't. (*In a whisper.*)

MOLLY. Yes, I would, my lad. You can add some jokes of your
own and lead the laughter, but you'll never see me again,
except from a great distance.

There is a pause. OLIVER *sits upright, staring at* MOLLY.

MOLLY. Oh Oliver, why do you get like this?

OLIVER. But I love you, I love you.

MOLLY. That's all right darling. You may love me. I want you to.

OLIVER. But I can't stand it when I'm not with you, when you're
in here talking to her, or go into his room to talk to him, and I
don't know what's going on, but I think of you and him
touching you and I don't know, what am I to do, Moll. You
see, before it was like — it was like I was stuck somewhere

underground and — and you took me out — and now I want to
be out all the time, but when you're not there it's like being
stuck back down again. (*Little pause.*) Last night you said I
was your husband even. But I'm not, am I? He is, isn't he? He
has you most.

MOLLY. But you have far more of me, especially now. He
doesn't kiss me where you kiss me, he doesn't hold me as you
hold me — we mustn't grudge him anything, Ollie. Not
anything. (*Little pause.*) Darling.

OLIVER (*looks at her*). I'm sorry for what I said. I didn't mean
it.

MOLLY. I know. (*Puts her arms around him.*) Oh my Ollie.

OLIVER. You still love me then, don't you?

MOLLY. Of course I do.

OLIVER. You won't ever send me away, will you?

MOLLY. When Rosie Hitchins from Guildford comes to claim you
back.

OLIVER. Never!

MOLLY. Well, not if I can help it.

OLIVER. Then I've got you, then, haven't I? (*Jubilant.*) Got you!

*They embrace. MOLLY kisses him tenderly, as if he were a
child. She wipes his cheeks with her fingers, then kisses him
again. The kiss becomes passionate. OLIVER puts his hands on
MOLLY's breasts, sighs.
MOLLY responds.*

OLIVER. Please Moll. Come out.

MOLLY (*steps away*). You're quite impossible, Oliver Treefe.
(*Laughs.*)

OLIVER. You will, won't you?

MOLLY (*hesitates*). Oh why not — yes — let's —

*There is a knock on the door, left. MOLLY looks at the door.
Another knock.*

MOLLY. Come in

EVE (*enters*). Excuse me. I wasn't sure whether you'd gone.

MOLLY. Oh, that's all right, darling. We're just off.

EVE. I wondered if I could have a few words with you.

MOLLY. Of course. Oliver, wait in the car, would you. I won't be a minute.

OLIVER *glances suspiciously at* EVE, *exits.*

EVE. I think it would be better if I left as soon as possible. So I'd be grateful if you got back by five. I'd like to catch the six o'clock train.

MOLLY. Would you like Oliver to drive you to the station?

EVE. No thank you. I'll call for a taxi, if I may.

MOLLY. Where are you going?

EVE. To Gosport.

MOLLY. I didn't know you had anyone in Gosport.

EVE. A niece.

MOLLY. And does she have children?

EVE. Yes.

MOLLY. You'll be able to help her with them, I suppose.

EVE. They're quite grown up.

MOLLY. Those are the ones that really need your help. (*Smiles.*)

EVE. If Teddy wakes I shan't say anything, I'd rather you explained.

MOLLY. He'll miss you dreadfully. So will I, of course.

EVE. I'll pack now. (*Goes towards the door, left.*)

MOLLY (*hesitates, then*). Evie.

EVE *stops, turns.*

MOLLY. Evie, please don't go! (*Runs across to her, embraces her.*) I need you so. I do.

EVE *stands stiffly for a moment, then turns, embraces* MOLLY.

EVE. Oh Moll!

MOLLY. You won't leave me, Evie. Will you?

EVE (*after a moment*). No Moll. Not if you really need me.

MOLLY. Oh thank you darling. Thank you. Thank you.

There is a sudden thumping from above. There is a pause. There is a honk from off, right.

TEDDY (*off, above*). Hey Molly, Eve — hey!

MOLLY *looks at* EVE *appealingly*.

EVE. You'd better go. But I can't tell lies for you, Molly
Treadley. I can't do that.

MOLLY. No, darling. I know.

Goes out through conservatory.
EVE *watches her go through conservatory, stands for a
moment. Puts her hand to her forehead.*
TEDDY *enters, left. He is wearing dressing-gown, slippers, but
is without a hearing-aid.*

EVE (*turning*). Teddy — You shouldn't be up.

TEDDY. Where's Moll?

EVE (*slowly and loudly*). She's gone out.

Sound of the car screeching down the drive.

TEDDY. She went out this morning — where's she gone to this
time?

EVE (*hesitates*). Oh, just for a drive.

TEDDY. What?

EVE. To get your drops. Teddy, you mustn't stay down here —
(*Goes over to him.*)

TEDDY. What? (*Irritably, pulling his arm away.*) Did she forget
them this morning, then?

EVE. They had to make up a fresh batch — it's too cold for you
down here, Teddy.

TEDDY. Not going back to bed with a stuffed nose — like being
in a damned prison. (*Goes over, pours himself a Scotch, slops
the drink, pays no attention, takes a gulp.*) Can't taste the
taste, only the heat. (*Sits down.*) Go in the car?

EVE. Yes. (*Goes back, sits down.*)

TEDDY (*after a pause*). Saw them coming around the side of the
house the other afternoon. Looked out of my window and
there they were, around my side of the house, right beneath
me. Like a pair of ghosts. (*Attempts to sniff.*) Don't worry, not
delirious, Evie. Like ghosts because I couldn't hear them.
Couldn't have smelt them either, come to that. Lost my
hearing, now I lost my smelling, what goes next, eh? (*Laughs.*)

She was laughing. He had his mouth open. Maybe shouting a
joke or something. Anyway, his mouth was open.

EVE. I think he has adenoids.

TEDDY. Great sense of humour?

EVE. No, adenoids.

TEDDY. Knocked on my window, but they didn't hear. Went
right on round. A moment later they were back again, on the
other side, gravel showering every which way. Too damned
fast. (*Pause.*) Too damned fast. God knows what he gets up to
when I can't see him. (*Pause, sniffs.*) Why didn't you tell her
yesterday I was running out, you could see I was, couldn't you?

EVE. I'm sorry.

TEDDY. What you knitting there, a coloured ladder?

EVE. A scarf.

TEDDY. What?

EVE (*explosively*). A *scarf!* It's going to be a scarf.

TEDDY. Like having him around the house all the time?

EVE. Who?

TEDDY. What's he like?

EVE. Oh, I expect he's a normal boy.

TEDDY. What?

EVE. A normal boy.

TEDDY (*after a pause*). Hey Evie — (*pause*) last night —
(*sniffs*) you tuck me up in bed? Or was it a dream?

EVE. I made your bed comfortable for you. The covers had
slipped.

TEDDY. Oh. (*Little pause, then vaguely.*) What? (*Attempts to
blow his nose.*) Damn! Damn! (*Sits, sunken in misery.*)

EVE (*looks at* TEDDY, *goes on with her knitting, looks at*
TEDDY, *then suddenly*). Get rid of him, Teddy!

TEDDY (*looks at her. Pause*). What?

EVE *gets up, goes over to him, takes out the bottle of drops,
hands it to* TEDDY.

EVE. I can't bear to see you suffering like this.

TEDDY. That's all right, Evie, anyone can make a mistake. (*Takes the bottle, administers the drops, two to each nostril.*)

    EVE *goes back, sits down.*

TEDDY. Tell me something, Evie — that scarf. Is it for me?

EVE. Yes.

TEDDY. Thank you Evie.

    There is a pause. TEDDY *sits staring ahead.* EVE *goes on with her knitting.*

TEDDY. What? (*Dimly.*)

    Lights.

Scene Two

A couple of hours later. TEDDY *is sitting, staring ahead, as before.*
EVE *is knitting.*
TEDDY *gets up, goes with his glass over to the cocktail cabinet, pours himself another large Scotch.*
EVE *looks up towards him then goes on with her knitting.*
MOLLY *enters through the conservatory, followed by* OLIVER.

MOLLY (*stops, stares at* TEDDY, *looks at* EVE). Darling, should you be up, Gracey said a few more days in bed —

TEDDY. Got tired of being stuck up there in bed — thought I'd come down, I'm fine — hello there boy, how are you?

OLIVER. Sir.

TEDDY. What?

OLIVER. All right, thank you, sir.

TEDDY. What about a drink? Moll? (*Dashes some gin into a glass, hands it her.*)

MOLLY. But darling —

TEDDY. Where you been?

MOLLY. Oh, just out for a little drive —

TEDDY. What?

MOLLY. For a little drive.

TEDDY. Get my drops?

MOLLY. No, I got you a fresh bottle this morning —

TEDDY. Don't need them anyway, Evie had a bottle all the time — nice drive?

MOLLY. Except for a horrid little scene on the way back.

TEDDY. What?

MOLLY. A horrid little scene.

TEDDY. You and him?

MOLLY. No darling, two louts shooting in the field past the bridge. I made Oliver stop the car and when we went over there was a rabbit, they'd only wounded it and tied its legs, can you believe? and a beastly little dog —

OLIVER. A terrier.

TEDDY. What?

OLIVER. A terrier, sir.

TEDDY. No good boy, yours is the voice I'll never catch.

MOLLY. Anyway, they just stood there while Oliver had to kill it with a stick.

TEDDY. Killed the dog with a stick.

MOLLY. No, a rabbit, darling —

TEDDY. Rabbit, eh? Bet she didn't like that, eh boy?

OLIVER. No sir.

TEDDY. Doesn't like animals being hurt, do you Moll? Ever told you about the seals at Nanaimo, she wrote a song about it, got done across Nova Scotia because Bob Hoskins was a friend of mine, I asked him to do it for her. A good friend. (*Laughs*.) Eh Moll? But she'd never ever been to Nanaimo, eh Moll, but somebody told her about the seals and she made up a song out of her head, and that's how it got heard right across Nova Scotia. Nanaimo's in British Columbia, four thousand miles away — What do you think of that, eh Ollie — these ladies, seals, rabbits, songs — all the same to them, hey boy? Out in Nova Scotia we only shoot rabbits when we can't find any Catholics. We like to shoot Catholics. (*Laughs*.) Ever told you about that Moll? When some damned fool out hunting saw the bushes move, fired into them, wounded another damned fool hunting. Nova Scotia paper headlined the story, 'Father of

Nine Shot. Mistaken for rabbit.' Hey. Nine kids, that's how
we knew he was a Catholic. (*Laughs*.) Wish we'd had you
around, boy, to beat him to death with a stick.

MOLLY *has lit a cigarette.*

Hey girl, come over here. Come on.

MOLLY *looks at him.*

Come on, girl. Here, I say.

MOLLY *goes over to* TEDDY.

How many's it been, eh? How many seen her smoke,
boy? Two hundred, three hundred, since I was laid up — say
five, let you off with five, Molly, eh — one — two — three —
four — five — (*Smacking at her bottom.*) There, letting you off
lightly, eh girl.

OLIVER'*s face is set.*

MOLLY (*seeing* OLIVER'*s face*). Evie, is there some tea for Oliver.

EVE (*gets up*). Come with me, Oliver. (*Goes out, back.*)

TEDDY. Hey boy, something I've been meaning to ask you —
that hedge you started, remember seeing you at it on my way
to the ditch I fell into — how's it going, got it level?

OLIVER. Well, I've been doing a lot of driving. Haven't had a
chance to get back to it yet.

TEDDY. Don't know what you're saying, boy, but I can see from
your face it's an excuse, where's Mr Goldberg's Alvis, put it
away?

OLIVER. Sir.

TEDDY. Where?

OLIVER. In the garage, sir.

TEDDY. Give me the keys, boy.

MOLLY. Darling, I did say Oliver could give his Dad a run later
this evening —

TEDDY. The keys. (*Holds out his hand.*)

OLIVER *takes the keys out of his pocket, glaring at* TEDDY.

TEDDY. That's the boy. Now why don't you go trim the hedge
until the sun sets — eh? (*Gives him a friendly cuff on the
shoulder.*)

MOLLY. But he hasn't had tea —

TEDDY. What? (*Turns around, gives her a malevolent stare.*)

MOLLY. He hasn't — (*Stops.*)

TEDDY. Well? (*Looks at* OLIVER.)

> OLIVER *turns, blunders into the conservatory.*

> Hey, just a minute —

> OLIVER *picking up shears.*

There's another thing, don't need you around the house at night any more, you can go back to your Daddy now, best if you move out this evening, eh?

> OLIVER *stands staring at* TEDDY, *then turns, goes off.*

(*Turns.*) Tell you the truth, Moll, don't like him. Foxy little face. Have you noticed his foxy little face?

MOLLY. No.

TEDDY. Just what you said when we took him on — furtive, pasty, crooked —

EVE (*appears at the back*). Oliver's tea is ready.

> *There is a pause.*

TEDDY. Oh, hey Eve, that boy, he's not going to be around at night — just told him to go home to his Daddy.

EVE. Oh.

TEDDY. Come and have one of your dry-as-dust sherries, Evie. (*Goes to the cocktail cabinet.*) Things are getting back to rights here, going to get Moll to play us one of her tunes in a minute —

EVE. That'll be nice — (*Advancing.*)

MOLLY (*to* EVE). Would you please leave us. (*Low.*)

TEDDY. What?

> EVE *goes towards door, left.*

> Hey, Evie, where are you going?

> EVE *exits.*

> What's the matter with her?

> *There is a pause.*

TEDDY. Hey Moll? Hey?

They stare at each other.

MOLLY. Why did you do that?

TEDDY. What?

MOLLY. I've never known you humiliate a child before.

TEDDY. What?

MOLLY. Never known you humiliate a child before. (*Loudly, fiercely.*)

TEDDY. Oh. (*Pause.*) Never had one to humiliate before. (*Laughs, then turns, goes and sits down.*)

MOLLY (*watches him, then runs to him*). Oh Teddy — what is it, what is it?

TEDDY *looks at her, turns his head away, mutters something.*

MOLLY (*kneels, takes his hand*). You're still not well, you shouldn't be up, darling — please come to bed —

TEDDY. What? What? What? (*Pause.*) Faces are different when they shout at the deaf. Ever thought of that, what I have to see in your faces — swelling, with effort and — contempt. And a little trickle of noise comes out I have to make sense of. Most often I get it wrong. I can see that in your faces too. Bellowing, contempt and boredom. That's all I see on your faces, all there is to see, isn't anything else, I see what's there. Everything. All I have of my own is — is the smell of fish. Fish. Know what's ahead of me — think I don't. I've seen old men. Hate this country of yours. Small and damp like a prison. Shambling, shambling about — cocktail cabinet to arm-chair, arm-chair to cocktail cabinet, pyjamas bagging out around the arse, crutch stained with pee dribble, cocktail cabinet to lavatory to arm-chair, to — to — Eve tucking me in, like I was a kid — teeth out in a glass — and all the time your faces swelling and bellowing, boredom and contempt, hate it, hate it, hate you all — what you've done to me — why didn't you leave me alone, never needed you, don't need you, natter, natter, natter — (*Sits staring ahead.*) Brought me here to die. Know you. Know what you are. (*Sits staring ahead, shrunken and malevolent.*)

MOLLY. Omigod!

TEDDY. What? (*Laughs.*) Ha! Look — there he is — back — look

at him — little — (*Gets up, goes over to the conservatory.*)
Get up!

OLIVER *rises. He is holding the shears.*

Hah! You're fired boy! Fired! Mine. Belongs to me. Mr
Goldberg's Alvis too — do what I like with her — everything —
you're fired, fired — (*Spits into* OLIVER's *face, laughs, turns,
goes to chair, sits down with his back to* OLIVER, *looks at*
MOLLY *laughs.*)

OLIVER *stumbles towards* TEDDY.

MOLLY. Don't, don't, omigod — don't — don't —

OLIVER *thrusts the shears into* TEDDY's *neck, again and again.*
TEDDY *lurches back, blood spouting.*

MOLLY. Omigod — omigod — (*Goes to* TEDDY.)

OLIVER. Didn't mean it, didn't mean it, Miss — he made me —
made me — what'll I do — (*pause*) Miss!

OLIVER *drops the shears, turns, runs out through
conservatory.*

MOLLY (*Looks at* TEDDY). Poor Teddy. Poor old man. (*Pause.*)
Omigod! Omigod! (*Goes to him, puts her arms around him.*)

Eve! Eeee-eeve! Eee-ve!

After a pause, EVE *enters.*

MOLLY. Eee-eeve! (*Sees her.*) He's alive, he's still alive; get
help you fool! Get help!

Lights.

Scene Three

About an hour later. TEDDY's *body has been removed.*
GREAVES *and a PC are standing, whispering.*

EVE (*enters, left*). It's just as I said. She's asleep. Dr Gracey gave
her a very strong sedative. There's not the slightest chance
you'll be able to see her until the morning.

GREAVES. Then perhaps you'll answer a few questions, Miss Mace.

EVE. I'm afraid I can't. I must get back to Mrs Treadley.

GREAVES. But if she's asleep?

EVE. Dr Gracey asked me to sit by her. She was in a state of shock. And if she wakes —

GREAVES. Miss Mace, I don't quite understand your position in the household.

EVE. I'm — the companion-housekeeper.

GREAVES. I see. And are you the only staff?

EVE. Well, there's a boy from the village, to help with the gardening and drive the car from time to time.

GREAVES. And was he here when the accident happened?

EVE. No. He'd gone home.

GREAVES. So there was just you, and Mr and Mrs Treadley?

EVE. Yes.

GREAVES. And did you see the accident?

EVE. No. I was in the kitchen.

GREAVES. So Mr and Mrs Treadley were alone in here?

EVE. Yes. Now I really must —

GREAVES. Where are the shears?

EVE. The shears?

GREAVES. Dr Gracey said the wound had been caused by gardening shears.

EVE. Oh. Oh yes — they're in there. On the second shelf under the potato sacking.

GREAVES. Why?

EVE. Because that's where they belong.

GREAVES. But they must have been covered in blood.

EVE. Of course they were. I washed it off.

GREAVES. But that was important evidence.

EVE. Evidence of what? It was an accident. Now I really must go to Mrs Treadley — you can come back tomorrow.

MOLLY (*enters, in night-dress and dressing-gown*). Ee-eeve —
(*Stops.*) Oh, who are you?

EVE (*crosses to her*). Molly — you shouldn't be up, you must get
back to bed.

MOLLY. Who are they?

GREAVES. Police, Mrs Treadley, I wonder if we could —

EVE. They were just leaving. Now come along —

MOLLY. The police. Oh I'm so glad you've come, I want to make
a complaint.

EVE. Molly —

MOLLY. No, darling, I'm going to. About those ambulance
men. They were rough — far too rough — I told them to be
careful, but one of them pushed me away, yes, actually
pushed me, didn't he Evie, when I was trying to help them
lift him — and then they said he was dead but he wasn't, not
until they came and heaved him about and wouldn't let me —
he was alive, wasn't he Evie. I know because I held him you see,
and I could feel something pumping under his blood, quite
strongly, there was life in him and then they came — it must
have been them, something they did — and they were very rude
too, weren't they, Evie, do you know they refused to let me
ride to the hospital with him, my own husband and they
refused — so I want to report them, will you report them for
me?

GREAVES. I shall certainly question them, Mrs Treadley.

MOLLY. Will you? Oh thank you — thank you, you're very —
would you like a drink?

GREAVES. No thank you, Mrs Treadley.

MOLLY. What about you, I'm sure you'd like one, wouldn't you?

GREAVES. We're not allowed to drink on duty, Mrs Treadley.

EVE. Now come my dear — back to bed —

MOLLY. No, no, just a minute, Evie, I'd like a — I can't sleep you
know — it's no good — I've tried and tried — you're sure you're
not allowed — will you excuse me if I just have a little, teeny
weeny — (*Goes to drink.*)

EVE. You really mustn't drink — Dr Gracey gave you a sedative —

MOLLY. Well, it hasn't worked darling, has it, I mean here I am

full of beans, God knows what he gave me, unless it was beans
of course — (*laughs*) and wasn't he so incompetent, he
really was, not that I want to get him into trouble, he's old and
easily upset, all he could do was shake those dreadful wattles
of his, he had no idea, no idea at all. I can't help thinking if
we'd got a younger man Teddy might still be — someone who
could stand up to those ambulance bullies and — but all poor
Gracey could do was shake his wattles and try to get me to bed,
oh — (*laughs*) I don't mean — of course not — (*stops*) but I
don't want to get him into trouble. Certainly not. He was very
good to Teddy's ears. (*There is a pause.*) Oh, I do feel — feel —
drinking by myself — do excuse me, but it's been a bit of a —
a bit of a —

GREAVES. Would you mind telling me how it happened, Mrs
Treadley.

MOLLY. What?

EVE. You can't possibly ask her questions — you can see the state
she's in. Now come, Molly, I insist —

MOLLY. Oh tush tush, Eve, tush, I'm perfectly all right, perfectly.
And I want to — to help these men — now what was it you—?

GREAVES. How did it happen, Mrs Treadley?

MOLLY. What?

GREAVES. How was Mr Treadley killed?

EVE. Molly, don't —

MOLLY. But it was an accident. Surely you know —
haven't you told them, Evie, it was nobody's fault — except
those men who were rough and poor old Gracey, it just —
just happened you see, didn't it, Evie?

GREAVES. But Miss Mace wasn't in the room at the time.

MOLLY. What? Oh — no, no, you weren't were you darling, she
generally comes in later, to clean up our messes for us, don't
you darling? (*Laughs.*)

GREAVES. You and Mr Treadley were alone.

MOLLY. What?

GREAVES. There was just you and Mr Treadley.

MOLLY. Oh. Yes. Yes, that's right. Me and Mr — Teddy. And the
cocktail cabinet, of course, that's always there, to make a third.

EVE. Molly — (*goes to her*) don't talk now. Don't talk now.

MOLLY. What, why darling, there's nothing to be afraid of, is there?

GREAVES. No, Mrs Treadley.

MOLLY. You see, it was just an accident. They understand that. That's all there is to it. (*Turns on radio. There is music playing.*)

EVE. Now Molly you're going to come with me —

GREAVES (*goes to* EVE, *and very quietly*). Miss Mace! Mrs Treadley has offered to help us in our enquiries. If you persist in interrupting. I shall have to ask you to leave the room.

MOLLY. What? (*Looks at* EVE.)

GREAVES. You were telling us what happened, Mrs Treadley.

MOLLY. Well, it was — something ghastly happened, you see. He had an accident. I — I didn't really see it, my back must have been turned or I was looking away for a moment but — but then there he was. Spurting — spurting — do you see?

GREAVES. One moment he was alive, and the next he was dying?

MOLLY. Yes — well, he had these sudden changes of mood recently, didn't he Evie? (*Laughs.*)

GREAVES *looks at* MOLLY. *There is a pause.*

MOLLY. Just a minute — need to — another little — a truth drink so you'll know I — (*Laughs, going to pour herself another drink, unsteady on her feet.*)

EVE (*goes over*). No, Molly — no — (*Attempts to take the bottle from her.*)

(*There is a short, absurd wrestle.*)

MOLLY. Bugger off, bitch!

EVE *recoils.*

MOLLY. Sorry Evie — sorry. Forgive please. Pretty please with sugar on it. (*Laughs, pours, then to* GREAVES.) That's all I have to say —

EVE (*to* GREAVES). This is disgraceful, disgraceful. I'm going to phone Dr Gracey and tell him —

GREAVES. That's your privilege, Miss.

MOLLY. What, she's got a pash on me, haven't you, Evie —

EVE *exits, left.*

MOLLY. Yes, she has, do you know about the pashes ladies have on ladies, ladies like her on ladies like me, are you married?

GREAVES. Yes.

MOLLY. Is she pretty, your wife?

GREAVES (*crosses to the radio, turns it off. Silence, then intimately.*) You were going to tell me the truth, Mrs Treadley.

MOLLY. What?

GREAVES. The truth.

MOLLY. What about?

GREAVES. Your husband's death. He was murdered, wasn't he?

MOLLY. Murdered? (*Pause. She yawns.*) I'm sorry — sorry — what?

GREAVES. Did you do it?

MOLLY. What?

GREAVES. You did, didn't you?

MOLLY. What — what do you do to people, when you — you catch them?

GREAVES. That's for the courts to decide.

MOLLY. But if they're children?

GREAVES. But there aren't any children, are there, Mrs Treadley?

MOLLY. Oh yes. Yes. We're all children in this house, all of us. That's what caused it, you see. But nobody meant — oh please believe — it wasn't mean't. He — he brought it on himself! He did! He did! An old man, come to the end, he wanted to die, he wanted to — full of hate — I couldn't bear his hate — and he knew — you see he knew — he was right, about his old man's smells, his deafness and the boredom, the boredom and the bellowing and the contempt and the pee-dribble and his pyjamas arsing — and — and —

GREAVES. And is that why you killed him, Mrs Treadley?

MOLLY. What?

GREAVES. Did you kill him?

MOLLY. I —

Pause.

EVE (*enters*). I've spoken to Dr Gracey. He's coming over —

MOLLY. It was her! She did it! She did it! (*Pause.*) No, no, sorry Evie, sorry darling — it was me. Yes. I killed him. I killed him. I took the things and I — I — (*Makes thrusting movements, stops abruptly.*) And now you all hate me, don't you, like the ambulance and Gracey and all — all hate me — well, here I am, look at me you — you — (*runs to* PC) what do you see, an old vamp, is that what you see, but you'd roger me, too, wouldn't you, I could make you love — I'm still — look — look — (*Makes to lift her night-dress to him.*)

EVE *strides across, grips* MOLLY *by the arm, pulls her away.* MOLLY *collapses against* EVE.

MOLLY. Bed now, Evie, bed please. Bed darling — —

Lights.

Scene Four

Some months later. Afternoon. The room fills with light, steadily, to bright sunlight. There are dust sheets over the sofa, the chairs. On the sofa, MOLLY's *scarf, handbag. The door, left, is open.* EVE *enters from the left, wearing a light raincoat. She goes to the handbag, begins to go through it.*
MOLLY *appears at the door, back. She is also wearing a light coat. She stands watching* EVE, *then comes across, takes the handbag from her.*

MOLLY. Thank you, darling. I do wish people would stop rummaging through it, it's been emptied and refilled by so many different ladies recently, police ladies, prison ladies, hospital ladies, (*takes out a cigarette*) it doesn't feel mine any more. (*Lights cigarette.*) What were you looking for, darling? The sleeping pills?

EVE. I couldn't remember whether we'd brought them.

MOLLY. Do we need them, though? Surely we don't mind being awake on an August afternoon? (*Takes a bottle out of the pocket.*) Do you want to look after them?

EVE. No, of course not, Moll.

MOLLY. Oh, you might as well, darling. I'm not going to try

again. For one thing, I don't seem to be very good at it, and I do hate the way they drag one back, with stomach pumps and sermons. Do take them, darling. There.

EVE (*takes them*). I'll make up a bed if you still want to lie down.

MOLLY. Lie down?

EVE. You said you had a headache.

MOLLY. Did I? Well then it's gone.

EVE. Oh. Oh good! Well, what about our walk then?

MOLLY. Our walk?

EVE. You were looking forward to a walk.

MOLLY. I think I'll leave it until tomorrow.

(*Pause.*)

To tell you the truth, darling, I'm a bit confused at finding everything so familiar.

EVE. It's my fault. I shouldn't have agreed to let you come back — at least so soon.

MOLLY. So soon? But I haven't been here for a long time. After such an eventful spring, and a summer wasted in — in institutions — I'd have hated to have missed the old haunts in their autumn colours. I long to see them.

EVE. You do want a walk then?

MOLLY. What do you want, Evie?

EVE (*intensely*). I want our old Moll back again.

MOLLY. Do you really? Our old judge found the old Moll a trifle too degenerate for his taste. Quite disgusting, in fact. Quite disgusting. Disgusting.

EVE. He had no right — no right to say those things. They had no right to make you go through that trial, not after — after the truth had come out. I shall never believe in British justice again.

MOLLY. Poor Eve! Still, think what we would have lost. The sight of old Treefe, for example, touching his forelock to thank everyone for all the trouble they were putting themselves to, to hang his son. Who's only just come of hangable age. (*Pause.*) Can I have a drink? No — no more drinks for me.

EVE. You must stop blaming yourself, Molly. You stood by him right to the bitter end.

MOLLY. Not quite, darling. His bitter end comes on Monday week, at six in the morning, isn't it? He's going to that without me. (*Pause*.) Looking across as if he believed I could just come out of my box and into his, and cuddle him through it. His peaky face, and the spot blooming on his nose. Do you think he'll expect me on Monday week, too, right to the very last, as a child expects his Mummy to come and take him away. (*Turns away*.) I'd have made a good mother, wouldn't I?

EVE. He did do it, Moll.

MOLLY. Of course he did. (*Pause, makes a violent gesture*.) So hang the little beggar! By the way, darling, I haven't thanked you properly for bringing him to book. Thank you. If it hadn't been for you —

EVE. I couldn't let you sacrifice yourself. I couldn't, Moll.

MOLLY. No. No. I don't suppose you could.

EVE. We have to do right by those we care about.

MOLLY. Yes. Yes we do. You love me Evie, don't you?

EVE. Yes.

MOLLY. Thank you.

EVE. Oh Moll — (*Gives a sudden shy smile*.)

MOLLY. It *is* a lovely afternoon, isn't it? Would you like a walk?

EVE. I'd love one.

MOLLY. Right. Off you go then.

They stare at each other.

Darling, we really must start doing our separate wants, or how shall we two live together? Please go darling. (*Pause*.) Please.

EVE *exits through conservatory*.

MOLLY (*after a pause*). Pretty please (*pause*) with sugar on it.

Lights.

Curtain.

MAN IN A
SIDE-CAR

Author's Note

I've forgotten every stage of writing *Man in a Side-Car* except its initiating image: the photograph in a newspaper of a young, pretty and already celebrated lady novelist, with her husband behind her elbow and a baby (or a cat) at her feet; that, and a subsequent report in probably the same newspaper that the marriage had broken up amicably. I suppose there were the routine drafts on drafts, but I don't recall even the usually memorable moment of completion. There was some fuss, though, when the play was sent out. Kenith Trodd, who had been involved in all my previous plays, first as script editor, then as producer, had left the BBC, probably in one of their periodic purges of talent, and no one there was sufficiently taken by *Man in a Side-Car* to offer it, except in a cursory way, to this or that director until Anne Scott, who had worked with Kenith Trodd and myself, rescued it from another producer's desk and brought it to the attention of James MacTaggart. To Anne Scott, then, my double thanks.

Because, in retrospect, the most important fact about *Man in a Side-Car* (for me, anyway) is that James MacTaggart directed it. We'd already worked together, some years before, on a small play of mine called *Pig in a Poke*, and got on sufficiently well to hope that we would again, some day. With *Man in a Side-Car* we went from getting on to friendship — we drank quite a few drinks together; had one or two small quarrels; and laughed a great deal — and professionally, had moved from clearly defined roles as author and director to rather more than trusting collaborators. So when I read through the play the other day to check it out for publication, I was still quite unable to separate the text from my (seven or so years later) vivid recollection of James's realization of it. In fact, it now seems so inextricably his work as well as mine, that in offering it up I feel that I am withholding rather more than simply his half. But then Gerald Savory or someone like him wiped the tape, of course. And now James is dead; and all I can do is dedicate the lesser half to his memory, in gratitude and continuing admiration.

MAN IN A SIDE-CAR was first broadcast by the BBC as Play for Today on 27 May 1971. The cast was as follows:

EDITH	Gemma Jones
GERALD	James Laurenson
TOMMY	David Collings
MRS MERCHANT	Sheila Beckett
DAVID	Geoffrey Matthews
HELEN	Yvonne Gilan
DR SLOKUM	Walter Horsburgh
GILES	Jonathan Lawson
WAITRESS	Tessa Lander
MEN IN COFFEE BAR	Roger Minnis, Steve King, Colin Richmond, Paul Barton
GIRLS IN COFFEE BAR	Monica Wilding, Rosemary Turner
THREE MEN IN HOSPITAL	Len Sanders, Bert Simms, Ernest Jennings
TWO NURSES	Constance Reason, Iris Fry
WARD ORDERLY	Leonard Kingston

Directed by James MacTaggart
Producer Graeme McDonald
Script Editor Ann Scott
Designer Stuart Walker

Act One

1. Interior Edith's Study. Day. *It is a sparsely furnished room, with one picture, mediaeval and devotional, on the wall. There is a desk beside a window. The window looks out onto a path which is, in fact, a narrow drive. The drive curves around a bend and then onto a country road. The desk is an old-fashioned school desk, with a sunken ink-well and a ridge for a pen. EDITH is writing into an exercise book at the desk. She uses a fountain pen that she dips into the ink-well. To her left is a pile of five exercise books, filled. Beside her, and behind her, past the window, is a bookshelf on which are arranged exercise books and novels. She is dressed in a long (as opposed to fashionably maxi) skirt, has hair swept down the side of her face, and in her cell-like room gives off a distinctly nun-like effect. She is in her early thirties. She is writing quickly and neatly onto the page, and at regular intervals is dipping her pen into the ink-well.*
EDITH's *voice over, as she writes:*

EDITH (*voice over*). Mathilda began to discover that she had many things against Simon, and consequently and quite consciously began to develop a proportional esteem for herself. For example, Simon had begun to take instruction with a view to conversion. He approached his studies — for that was what he had made of the matter — with an academic devotion that was as inelegant as it was thorough, and spoke of the impending moment at church as if he were about to be awarded a prize for an achievement, an advanced degree for example. Mathilda, who had gone over to Rome at the age of thirteen because she was in love with a girl, half Italian, half Irish, wholly beautiful and almost twelve, at her second boarding school, took her own Catholicism so much for granted that she could afford to be witty at its expense. Poor Simon was frequently shocked by her little jokes, and the resulting strain between them — a strain that confirmed Mathilda in her growing sense of independence — led to some strange failures in bed. These

failures were, of course, entirely Simon's. Mathilda, secretly
enjoying them, marked them up as victories. Simon might well
entitle himself to an adjoining pew, but his head would soon
rest uneasily on the adjoining pillow.

EDITH *smiles as she writes the last few sentences.*
Cut to *her face, then as the smile stiffens, cut to* the window
beside *her.*
GERALD, *in goggles, a flowing scarf, gauntlets, and a very
distinctive and expensive-looking leather coat with enormous
buttons, is staring in at her. He turns, walks away.*
EDITH *turns slowly, as if sensing him there, a second after he
has disappeared, frowns slightly, then goes back to her writing.*

It turned out, in fact, that Simon, who in the early days of their
relationship, had so amused himself by making fun of her own
small aspirations, was unable to see the comedy of his own,
larger ones. She came to the conclusion and not at all
reluctantly that her husband was a fraud. She saw, with only
enough pain to spicen the recognition into anticipation, that
there was little prospect of their marriage lasting the course.
She was too clever by half. Indeed, she was too happy by —

*Her voice is interrupted by the explosive sound of the motor-
bicycle starting.*
EDITH's *shoulders jump, her pen waits above the paper as the
motor-bike roars off.*

Her voice over, writing.

— by more than half.

2. Exterior. The path from the cottage. Day. GERALD *on his
motor-bicycle, which has an old-fashioned side-car. It roars around
the bend, and out of sight, and as it does so:*
MRS MERCHANT *wheeling a pram, comes into shot. She is staring
after the motor-bike.*

3. Interior. Edith's Study. Day. EDITH *is now nearly at the
bottom of the page. She writes:*

EDITH (*voice over*). She knew the day would come when
she would say to her child-bridegroom — 'If you were half a
man, you would go.' And she equally knew that, being half

a man, he would. So many divisions could be made to make a very simple sum.

She turns the page, shot of *the blank page, her pen hovers, then writes:*

But Simon, if he was not capable of success, was finding the consolations of malice. He —

EDITH *smiles, screws the top back on her pen, puts it in the ledge, closes the ink-well, blots the page, closes the exercise book, then goes out of the study.*
Follow her *as she enters:*

4. Interior. Gerald's Study. Day. EDITH *enters* GERALD's *study. There is a desk, a typewriter, a camp-bed, unmade, books, papers, etc, scattered everywhere.*
There is an ash-tray full of cigarette ends, a pair of spectacles, a pipe half-smoked, an open box of cheroots, and beside the typewriter various sheets of papers, some with fragments of typing on them. There is a sheet in the typewriter.
EDITH *makes a face, goes to the window, opens it, then goes out. Comes back in, looks down at the page, reads a few lines, goes out again, and* follow her *to the kitchen.*

5. Interior. The kitchen. Day. *First* come in on MRS MERCHANT's *face, smiling, then* cut back to EDITH, *smiling, and she blocks the view for a second, then turns around, having lifted* GILES *out of his highchair, and is now cuddling him.*
GILES, *who is about nine months old, not seen until that instant.*

6. Exterior. A Railway Station. *The motor-bike.* GERALD *appears with* TOMMY.
TOMMY *is wearing a slightly ludicrous, very long, tatty overcoat. He is carrying an equally tatty overnight bag.*
They come to the motor-bike; GERALD *fishes into the side-car, hands* TOMMY *a pair of goggles and crash helmet, they get in and on respectively.*

7. Exterior. Country Roads. GERALD *is driving as:*
Credits.

Follow them through country roads, and on them in different shots, some of GERALD in close-up. Some of TOMMY, some from in front, some from behind, fading on the two of them in shot advancing as credits fade.

8. Interior. The kitchen. Day. EDITH *is holding the bottle for* GILES, *while also drinking a cup of tea.* MRS MERCHANT *is eating a proper lunch, as the noise of the motor-bike outside.* EDITH *glances up, then goes on feeding* GILES.
Sound of voices and TOMMY's *laughter outside the back door, then* GERALD *and* TOMMY *enter, still in goggles and helmets.*

TOMMY. Well, hello then.

He comes around, gives EDITH *a kiss, bends down, clucks at* GILES.

GERALD, *meanwhile is taking off his gear, smiling at* EDITH. GILES *begins to cry.*

EDITH. Your goggles.

TOMMY. Oh.

He takes his goggles off.

GERALD. No, it's because you've taken the bottle away.

EDITH *glances at him, puts the bottle down on the table.*

TOMMY (*to* GILES, *who is still crying*). What is it, Giles, what's the matter, don't you recognise me then, you only saw me yesterday.

EDITH. Yes, but he cried then, too.

She picks GILES *up, looks at* MRS MERCHANT, *who gets up; they go out together.*

TOMMY. It was wind yesterday.

GERALD. Don't worry, I don't believe they *know*.

TOMMY *sits down, cutting himself some bread.*

TOMMY. He never cries at me, normally.

He shakes his head, worried.

GERALD. For Christ's sake — he's not going to throw you out. Well?

TOMMY. What? Oh, well like I said, they're interested Gerald, certainly, the only thing that's holding them back, likely, is they're waiting to see the second act complete. (*He eats ravenously.*) That's all.

GERALD. Did they have any constructive suggestions?

EDITH *comes back into the room.*

TOMMY. I hope you don't mind, Edie — (*Holding up the bread.*)

EDITH. Please.

Neutrally, she begins to clear up.

(*To* GERALD.) Do you want anything?

GERALD. Just some sense.

TOMMY. Well — well, no, well he liked it, Gerrie. (*To* EDITH.) That's Humphrey Jones, Edie, I worked with in Cardiff I mentioned to you who's got hold of that new theatre club in Chiswick, he's a smart bastard — no, all he said (*back to* GERALD) was he liked its *tone* and that when we got it worked through to the curtain to let him be the first to refuse.

GERALD *laughs.*

You know what I mean, first *refusal* he wants, it's the next thing to an option. Edie, could I have one of those yogurts if you've got one?

He turns around in a practised way, opening the fridge, takes out a yoghurt.

EDITH. But he's not taking an option?

TOMMY. Well I couldn't insist on it could I as — I'm a friend, see.

EDITH (*ironically*). Well, that's all right then.

GERALD. What does that mean?

TOMMY *is spooning down the yogurt at great speed.*

EDITH. The director of a new theatre's likely to find himself with a lot of new friends as well. Or would he make it a principle to buy options on the work of strangers only?

GERALD. Where's Giles?

EDITH. Having his nappy changed.

GERALD. Mrs Merchant doing it?

EDITH (*pretends to think*). Unless he's doing it himself.

TOMMY. But what really matters is that I could see he was excited by it, he wouldn't pretend over that, you know —

He is watching GERALD, *who gets up, picks up the overnight bag, and goes out.*

(*To* EDITH.) He's not a complete bastard.

EDITH. Merely a clever one.

She looks at TOMMY *who is smiling slightly shiftily. There is a pause.*

TOMMY. Um, I was wondering, could you spare — ?

EDITH. Please.

TOMMY *turns around, opens the fridge, takes out another yogurt.*

What is it about?

TOMMY. What? Our play? Hasn't Gerrie told you?

EDITH. No. Nor have you.

TOMMY. Well, you never asked before. (*Laughs.*) I mean, I assumed . . .

He opens the yogurt, begins eating.

EDITH. Well?

TOMMY. Well. (*Laughs.*) It sounds very modish in outline, you know. (*Pause.*) Well . . . (*He laughs again.*)

EDITH. I like quite a few of the current modes.

TOMMY. Well, in fact it's about these four queers who ran a butcher's shop. Two of them draggy queens, see, and two of them butch —

EDITH (*poker-faced*). Butch Butchers.

TOMMY (*laughs desperately*). That's one we did cut out, no, you see, it's the sort of sexual and emotional permutations and combinations — well, it's all in the dialogue and the tone, see, there's no plot as such, but if it's played in the right style it could be something special. (*Little pause.*) A cross between Racine and Orton. (*Little pause.*) Not just another commercial camp-up, Edie.

EDITH. Ah. An uncommercial camp-up?

TOMMY. Oh, Edie! (*Little pause.*) Why are you being so depressing then?

EDITH. Self-protection.

TOMMY. For Gerald you mean?

EDITH. Actually, I meant for myself.

TOMMY. I'm sure it'll come off.

EDITH. Yes. Almost at once. If it gets on.

TOMMY. Well, I'm very hopeful.

EDITH (*stares at him unwinkingly*). Good.

TOMMY (*finishes his yogurt*). I must say, it's nice to be back. I've missed you all.

EDITH. You've only been away for the night.

TOMMY. Yes, well, it feels like a couple of weeks.

EDITH. Perhaps that's because it was going to be. A couple of weeks. We all adjusted to that prospect.

TOMMY. Oh? You didn't expect me back today then?

EDITH. No. Not actually.

TOMMY. But Gerald phoned last night — he left a message with Stewart to come back as soon as they'd read it at the theatre.

EDITH. Ah. In that case it must have been an emergency. (*She gets up.*)

TOMMY. Well, how's the novel going?

EDITH. I've done two days work, since you last asked.

TOMMY. Oh, good.

As EDITH *goes out.*

Humphrey Jones said he loved your last, to tell you especially.

EDITH (*reappears, smiles*). Oh, good. (*She waits.*)

TOMMY. Yes, he loved it. (*Rather feebly.*)

EDITH. Good.

She goes out, and as she does so TOMMY *wheels round to the fridge.*

9. Interior. Gerald's Study. Day. *He is sitting before the*

typewriter, spectacles on, staring down at the manuscript.
The over-night bag is at his feet.
EDITH *stands at the door.* GERALD, *pointedly, doesn't look up.*

EDITH. Can I speak?

GERALD (*still looking down*). You can.

EDITH. You summoned him back, then?

GERALD (*still looking down*). Yes.

EDITH. Why?

GERALD. I was getting bored.

EDITH. We did agree that we might try two weeks without him.

GERALD. Not quite. *You* said *you* could do without him. You asked me whether I could understand your feelings. I said I did. There was thus agreement about your feelings. None at all about policy.

EDITH. David and Helen are coming to dinner tonight. Or had you forgotten?

GERALD. On the contrary. I specifically mentioned it to Tommy, by way of an inducement.

As TOMMY *appears behind* EDITH.

Edith was wondering whether you could really face David and Helen tonight. I've been reassuring her.

TOMMY. No, I'm looking forward to it, who are they exactly?

GERALD. Her publishers. Manic depressers. But never mind — you'll have lots to eat. Edie'll make sure of that. And lots to drink. I'll make sure of that.

TOMMY (*grins*). Ahh, just what I need.

Close up of TOMMY's *face, beaming, seen from* EDITH's point of view, *then she goes out.*

10. Interior. Edith's Study. Day. EDITH *is at her desk, writing.*
See her from side, including a shot of the window.

11. Exterior. Garden. EDITH's point of view, *from her study window:*
MRS MERCHANT *is sitting in a deck chair, reading.*

12. Interior. Edith's Study. Day. *Throughout this, there's also the sound of a distant typewriter.*

EDITH (*writes, as voice over*). He was turning into a way of life with a strong moral point of view. Mathilda would have found this boring if she hadn't known, indeed cherished the knowledge that this was merely a stage towards something even less consequential. During his time with her he had abandoned everything in turn. He had abandoned his art, for which he had no talent; and then his religion, for which he had had no feeling, and then his love making for which he had had no desire. Shortly he would abandon failure, for which he had no stoicism, in favour of a more sensational posture.

There is the sound, dim, of GILES, crying.
EDITH *frowns, makes to write another sentence, then turns to the window, raps on it, points.*

13. Exterior. Garden. MRS MERCHANT, EDITH's point of view, *gets up, goes off screen.*

14. Interior. Edith's Study. Day. EDITH *turns back to her writing.*
Fade out.
In on EDITH *writing again.*

15. Exterior. Garden. MRS MERCHANT, EDITH's point of view, *playing with GILES, in his pram.*

16. Interior. Edith's Study. Day.

EDITH (*voice over*). Mathilda felt that although . . .

The typewriter stops.

. . . she had little time for Simon at the moment, she would manage to find some for his next phase. He promised, for a change, to be interesting. Also it would enable her to practise her newly acquired mercilessness, as well as to test her . . .

All this over, as sudden shouts of laughter from TOMMY and GERALD. She frowns, goes on writing, as the shouts continue . . .

17. Interior. Gerald's Study. Day. GERALD *and* TOMMY *are crouched on the floor playing tiddly-winks, with pennies and sixpences. Beside each is a pile of half-crowns.*
TOMMY *is playing.*
Come on them both from the door, then cut to:
TOMMY'*s face. Frowning in concentration as he is about to wink a tiddly into the pot. He does so, and then another one, very practised, extracts two half-crowns from* GERALD'*s pile, then moves back to do one a long way away, then shakes his head, moves forward to one closer in.*

GERALD. You're gutless, Tommy.

> TOMMY *pays no attention as he takes aim, very serious.*

For a quid?

TOMMY (*looks up*). Let's see it.

> GERALD *reaches into his pocket, takes out a pound, puts it between* TOMMY *and the cup.*

And if I miss?

GERALD. Oh, I never take anything from you, do I?

TOMMY. Done and done, boyo.

> *He crouches down, concentrating very hard.*
> *There is a sudden stillness, then he winks the tiddly in. He lets out a shout, reaches for the pound note.*
> GERALD *puts his foot down on the pound.*
> *See* GERALD'*s face smiling from* TOMMY'*s point of view.*
> TOMMY *crouching,* GERALD *standing above him.*

Oh, come on, Gerrie, it's mine, I won it.

GERALD. Not yet.

> GERALD *bends down, extracts the pound from under his shoe, holds it up, and as* TOMMY *reaches for,it, flicks it away from his fingers.*
> *He keeps this up for some time,* TOMMY *clutching,* GERALD *whipping away, until* TOMMY *suddenly closes on* GERALD; *they begin to wrestle, crashing about, clutching at each other half-laughing, half-gasping, until they roll to the floor.*
> TOMMY *has* GERALD *pinioned and is reaching for the pound, when*:

EDITH (*voice over. Focus on* TOMMY *and the pound*). I hate to disturb you, but could you make less noise please.

There is silence, then TOMMY *gets up grinning sheepishly. He
puts the pound note in his pocket.*

GERALD, *still on the floor, turns his head, grinning,
towards* EDITH.

TOMMY. Um. Oh I'm sorry, Edie, it was my fault entirely, we
had this idea about a wrestling scene, see, you know male
wrestling is all the vogue now, on stage and screen, of course,
we'll have it done in the nude, but we wanted to get . . .
wanted to get . . . (*He begins to laugh, helpless.*)

GERALD *still lies smiling, staring up at* EDITH.

(*Helplessly.*) Get — get I'm sorry, Edie. Sorry.

EDITH *looks at them both, turns, goes out.*
On TOMMY *and* GERALD.
TOMMY *is still laughing, his laughter dying down.*
GERALD *gets up, smiling.*
There is a pause, heavy, empty, then GERALD *turns, goes to
the desk, sits down.*
TOMMY *goes to the camp-bed.*
GERALD *sits staring at the typewriter.*

GERALD (*after a pause*). What about a drink?

TOMMY. Oooh.

18. Interior. The sitting room. Night. *A table, laid for dinner.*
DAVID, HELEN, TOMMY *and* GERALD *sitting or standing,
holding drinks.*
But come in first on TOMMY's *face, as he raises the glass to his
lips.*
He is already slightly tight.
Then take in DAVID *and* HELEN, *sitting rather stiffy, and then*
GERALD, *watching, smiling.*

TOMMY. No, no look (*expansively*) that the boys look like the
girls and the girls look like the boys in Cannabis Street or
Cannibal Street or wherever that doesn't matter, see, that just
gives us twice as many to fancy, doesn't it? Eh? (*He laughs.*)

HELEN *and* DAVID *join in.*

But you see uni-sex has been going on for years, yes it has,
in the States they've had those creature-ladies and blue-ringed
hair and goggles that are male martians, I'm sure of it, and in

Russia, you know, more elemental, they've gone in a straight
line with pills and operations, like that, to get the best of both
worlds, child-bearing muscle-men, what about, no I'm serious,
all of those shot-putters or putt-shotters and javelin throwers
and mile runners the authorities caught shaving in the bogs,
eh? Well, that's all right, who minds a bit of cheating in the
name of sport, but look, reverse it for a moment, think of it
this way, supposing yes supposing our test team, our fast
bowlers, were really women, eh? Supposing these South
African apartheid blokes were destroyed by an opening pair of
fast bowlers from Yorkshire who had little ladies' problems
and had to be rested for them, eh, well, wouldn't that be
lovely, we destroy the white man at cricket with our ladies
like we destroyed the black man with our ladies, eh? So what
happens then to white supremacy — like male supremacy,
down the flush bowl with it — (*Laughing.*)

HELEN *and* DAVID *also laugh.*
HELEN *gets up.*

Where are you going, Helen?

HELEN. I'm just going to see if Edith needs a hand.

TOMMY. Oh yes, oh that's good, what about our World Cup
side, eh, did it take a sex test, hormone count or whatever . . .

19. Interior. Kitchen. Night. EDITH *is mixing something on the
stove.*
HELEN *comes in.*

HELEN. Can I do anything?

EDITH (*suppressing slight irritation*). Oh no thanks. I'm fine.

HELEN. I must say, we're enjoying Tommy. He's terribly funny.

EDITH (*neutrally*). Ah — yes.

HELEN. He lives with you, does he?

EDITH. In a sense. He has done, off and on, since we were
students. We take him so much for granted we scarcely know
he's around.

HELEN. Gosh, I'd have thought that was quite difficult.

EDITH. Yes. It is.

HELEN. He's incredibly Welsh, isn't he?

EDITH. Sometimes. When he's had enough to drink.

HELEN (*after a pause*). David's terribly excited about your new one. He says it's nearly finished.

EDITH (*brightening*). Yes. Next month if I can keep it up — God willing, etc.

HELEN. I don't know how you manage.

EDITH (*laughs*). By becoming extremely selfish.

She takes a dish out of the stove.

20. Interior. Living-Room. Dinner table. Night. *They are seated around the table, but come in first on* TOMMY's *face, he is blinking slightly, and tighter.*
He raises the wine glass to his mouth, as GERALD *says:*

GERALD. Nappies.

DAVID. What?

GERALD. Didn't we decide you'd call it nappies. You said, 'Let's be brutal, that's what it's all about.'

DAVID (*doubtfully polite*). Nappies?

TOMMY (*laughing*). Brutally would be crappy nappies.

EDITH. There isn't a title.

DAVID. I must say, I'm rather relieved.

GERALD. But darling, didn't you — ah no, it was Giles that was all about nappies, brutally. I'm getting your children confused. (*To* HELEN.) Do *you* have any children? I always forget.

HELEN. Yes two actually.

GERALD. Two *actually*! As opposed to metaphorically — like Edith's novels. Do you enjoy them?

HELEN. Yes, of course. They're brilliant. They're my favourites.

GERALD. It's nice to hear someone being honest about their own off-spring.

HELEN *and* DAVID *laugh.*

HELEN. I thought you were talking about Edith's novels.

GERALD. Oh, do you think of them as your children, too?

EDITH. Helen was talking about her actual children, actually. As I think you've grasped.

There is a slight pause.

GERALD. Well, I certainly have now, haven't I? What do you enjoy about them, Helen? All they do is eat, defecate and sleep. Extremely enjoyable for the baby, but slightly disgusting for the rest of us.

DAVID. On the contrary. Babies are —

TOMMY. Why does Giles get that rash on his bum?

GERALD. It's their urine.

GERALD *passes* TOMMY *the wine.*
He fills his glass to the brim.

Acid in their urine.

EDITH. Could the rest of us have some please.

GERALD *looks at her, as if puzzled.*

GERALD. Oh the *wine* — I thought for a moment you meant —

TOMMY *erupts with laughter, as* GERALD *pours the wine around.*
After another pause, DAVID *says:*

DAVID. Tell me — I've often wondered — how do people write plays together. Do you alternate scenes, or what?

GERALD. Or what.

DAVID. What?

GERALD. Yes.

DAVID. I'm sorry.

GERALD. That's all right.

DAVID *laughs, clearly getting angry.*

DAVID. I'm afraid I don't understand —

TOMMY. What?

DAVID. I said I didn't understand.

GERALD. I'm sorry.

TOMMY. Why?

GERALD. He didn't understand.

TOMMY. What?

GERALD. How we write plays.

> Cut to EDITH's *face.*
> *She is watching* GERALD *and* TOMMY *through this, almost as if studying them.*

DAVID (*controlling himself*). Anyway, what it amounts to is that you've given up writing novels.

HELEN. Oh, did you . . . ?

> *She stops.*

GERALD. Writing novels ? (*As if astonished.*) What novels?

DAVID. Oh come on, I read it.

GERALD. Ah, my *novel.* I gave up writing that some considerable time before it was published.

EDITH. It was a good novel.

TOMMY (*emphatically*). It was a bloody good novel.

DAVID. Yes, I liked it.

> TOMMY *vaguely, and with seemingly no sense of context, says:*

TOMMY. Christ.

21. Interior. Living-room. Night. *They are all sitting around having coffees, and brandies, but* come in on GERALD, *smiling, as* TOMMY *says:*

TOMMY (*voice over*). No well you see it was like this . . . (*Falteringly.*) I was — she was a demi-vierge, can you credit of forty-three and a half, I think it was, and I was a raw boy of thirty-one precisely, well I didn't know what I was saying, excuse me a minute.

> *The sound of* TOMMY's *feet, stumbling.*
> *A door slamming.*

> Still on GERALD's *face as we* cut to *a shot of the group as a whole, evidently embarrassed, and then* cut to:

EDITH (*perfectly collected*). She could have stayed up. Got a Fellowship at Newnham. It never occurred to me she had a novel in her. Is it any good?

DAVID. Well, very accomplished and acceptably derivative.

> *Dreadful sounds off of* TOMMY *being sick.*

EDITH. Really? Derivative from?

HELEN. From you. I'd call it plagriarism.

More sounds from TOMMY.

DAVID. Let's just call it flattery.

GERALD *appears at the door.*

GERALD. Darling. (*Cheerfully.*) Where's the mop?

22. Interior. The Bedroom. Night. *A double bed, with a bedside table on either side. On* GERALD's *a reading lamp, a bottle of sleeping pills, and a pile of paper-back books, littered. On* EDITH's, *a reading lamp, and a baby-alarm. Also one book, 'Persuasion', with a book-marker in it. But none of this seen as yet. Come directly in on* EDITH's *face, she is staring up at the ceiling.*
The sounds of GILES' *breathing through the baby-alarm are audible but not yet explained. There are sudden little cries, followed by the heavy breathing.*
EDITH *moves her arm, and turns down the baby-alarm. As she does so,* GERALD *enters.*

GERALD (*beginning to undress*). He's lying down. I thought he was heroic the way he came back in and told that story against himself, didn't you? Do you think he gave them pleasure?

EDITH. About as much as he gave me, I should think.

Cut to *her face, as* GERALD *goes on undressing, off-screen.*

When did you start getting him drunk? This afternoon? (*Little pause.*) You know, you do go very well together. You're so predictable, like a rather silly married couple that everyone else has outgrown. How do you see yourself? As a *succès manqué?* Does he represent your last hold on your old self, attractive dominating, etc, and so forth?

GERALD *climbs into bed, lies down beside her.*

The glamour is entirely in the vocabulary. A failure. An unhappy husband. A desperate man. Try — flop. Flop's the right word for you. No Graham Greene connotations, no dimmed brightness, no forlorn flickers of promise. Flop. You're a flop and Tommy's a miserable despairing parasite. What the Americans call a bum.

23. Interior. Hall outside the bedroom. Night. TOMMY *is standing outside the door, listening. He is in a state close to collapse, exhausted.*

EDITH (*voice over*). What was interesting *and* poignant, about his performance tonight, was its desperation. Didn't you feel it? (*Sharply.*) Don't do that!

GERALD (*voice over*). Why not? We always used to celebrate the guests' departure with a spasm of analysis and a bout of love.

EDITH (*voice over*). What I'm celebrating tonight has nothing to do with you. In fact, that *is* what I'm celebrating. I witnessed Tommy's desperation and your malice this evening without even embarrassment. He was sad and you were trivial, and really I quite enjoyed it. Like recognizing a perfect definition. You behaviour was definitive. I said don't!

TOMMY *puts his hand to his forehead.*

24. Interior. Bedroom. Night. GERALD *is leaning over* EDITH, *grinning,* EDITH *is staring up. The sound of* GILES's *breathing is audible.*

EDITH. Would you please turn out the light. Because if you're going to go on grinning anally down at me, I'd rather not see you.

GERALD *maintains his position.*

You don't really think they're going to do your play, do you? Surely you know Tommy better than that. I do, anyway. He never showed it to them.

GERALD *goes on grinning down at her.*

What you've written is a flop. A flop's flop. And Tommy knows it.

GERALD. Do *you* know what I've got against you? Your chin. You've got the chin of a boxer. The tension of not punching it is driving me mad. I'd like to have you in the ring, belting away at your chin. Your novels stink. They make you lots of money and you sell the film rights, but they stink.

He rolls over, turns out the light.
There is a pause.

EDITH (*in the darkness*). Yes, but Tommy still didn't show your play to anyone. Not even a Welshman. He'll be leaving in the morning.

GERALD. Oh no he won't.

EDITH. Do you want a bet?

25. Interior. Gerald's Study. Night. TOMMY *is sitting on the camp bed. He begins to take off his shoes and socks. He looks forlorn, beaten. His hand moves, and he picks up a piece of bread, puts it into his mouth, chews on it desperately,* and on his face:

26. Interior. The Kitchen. Day. Come in on TOMMY's *face, munching, as if carried over from last scene.*

EDITH (*voice over*). You're a pig.

　　TOMMY *looks startled, then* cut to EDITH *looking down at* GILES, *to whom she is giving a bottle.*

TOMMY. And he'll grow up to be a big strong pig, like me, see.

　　EDITH *looks at him coolly, goes on feeding* GILES.

　　(*Clears his throat apprehensively.*) Um, while we're on the subject of pigs, Edie, in relation to myself see, I — well, I've been awake all night, worrying and guilty — I thought — (*attempts a charming smile*) — I'd outgrown that kind of thing, it must have been the train journey and being tired with it, you know.

EDITH. From here to Waterloo is thirty-five minutes.

TOMMY (*laughs*). Yes, that's true, well you know British Rail. (*Laughs.*) Anyway, I thought I had an apology to make.

　　Pause, he looks at EDITH, *who addresses herself to* GILES.

　　I did like your friends, very charming I thought they were. (*Pause.*) I hope I'm forgiven then.

　　EDITH *looks at him, makes as if to speak as:*

MRS MERCHANT (*comes through the door*). Good morning.

EDITH. Good morning. He's just finished.

　　Lifts him out of the chair, hands him to MRS MERCHANT.

MRS MERCHANT (*taking him*). And how's my ba-ba today? (*Carrying him out.*)

EDITH *suppresses a grimace of irritation.*

TOMMY. It's funny the way she talks to him like a sheep, eh? (*Laughs.*)

EDITH. You know I'm going to ask you to leave, don't you?

TOMMY *stares at her, licks his lips.*

It's time, Tommy. You've been with us since we started living together — and that was a year before we got married. Four years, interrupted by short breaks of three months or so, and your six months spell in Cardiff. Now I want you to go, and not to come back.

TOMMY (*staring at her helplessly*). But — Edie — because, you mean because of last night? I'll never — never — I promise —

EDITH. You see, you talk to me as if I were your older sister, or mother, someone you make promises to, that you're slightly frightened of, that will look after you and make everything all right again. (*She shakes her head.*) I don't feel protectively towards you. Not any more.

After a pause TOMMY *nods his head.*

TOMMY. Could I stay then until we've completed the play? It'll only be to impose on you another week or so? (*With dignity.*)

EDITH. Why? You know the play's no good. You didn't take it to anyone in London.

TOMMY. Do you think I'd lie about a thing like that?

EDITH. Yes. (*Smiles.*) Don't look so incredulous. You lie a great deal. About things like that, and more important things.

She gets up, comes over, stands behind him, touches his shoulder.

Just go, Tommy. Like a good boy. (*Both tenderly and ironically said.*)

TOMMY (*turns, clutches at her hand*). But what will I do — what?

The door opens.
EDITH *moves away from* TOMMY *as* GERALD *comes in.*

GERALD. Good morning.

27. Interior. Edith's Study. Day. EDITH *is watching* MRS MERCHANT *and* GILES.

28. Exterior. Garden. MRS MERCHANT *is wheeling* GILES *in the pram down the path.*

29. Interior. Edith's Study. Day. EDITH *turns, sits down at her desk, opens the exercise book, unscrews the top of her pen, dips it in the ink, makes as if to write. Her pen hovering over the page, as she reads the previous sentence:*

EDITH. . . . could not deny that the excitement the process of cleaning up gave her (*begins to write*) . . . was oddly pleasant, and although cerebral in its planning was becoming — was becoming — was becoming —

Lifting the pen up, she gazes down at the paper.

— cerebral in its planning was becoming —

She dips her pen into the ink, it hovers over the page.

— was becoming —

30. Interior. Gerald's Study. Day. TOMMY *is sitting on the bed, hands clasped between his legs.*
GERALD *is sitting at the desk-chair, doodling.*

GERALD. Why?

TOMMY. Because she told me to.

GERALD. I haven't. (*Little pause.*) What will you do? Go home to Llannelly?

TOMMY. No, I'll go to London.

GERALD. You've been to London.

TOMMY. I can always wash dishes for a bit.

GERALD. No you can't. Not any more.

TOMMY (*after a pause*). No.

GERALD. Where will you live?

TOMMY. Well, I can — perhaps I can go and stay with someone for a time, until I've settled down.

GERALD. No you can't. They won't have you. Not any more.

TOMMY. No.

GERALD. It's all ended, all that, Tommy. They're all married, to one sex or the other, they've got houses or flats, children or positions, one or two are even dead. They'd like to see you now for ten minutes in a pub, from an accidental meeting, and even so they won't ask you your address or give you theirs. There's nothing for you in London.

TOMMY (*after a pause*). And do you know, I can't do it anymore, I can't Gerrie. I'll tell you something: it frightens me, London. Not just the people who don't want to hear my voice when I telephone them, or the pubs nobody goes to any more, no, it's the whole place, the whole feel of the place and all eleven million of them, however many it is, it makes me feel too little.

GERALD. That's because you're too old. So what will you do, Tommy?

TOMMY. I don't know. I don't know. Of course Edie's right. I can't go on like this, living off you.

GERALD. Why not?

TOMMY. Because — (*thinks*) — she won't let me. (*Laughs.*)

GERALD. Well, there's always this, isn't there?

He holds up the manuscript.

Perhaps this will save you, if Humphry Jones is to be trusted.

TOMMY. But there's still the second act —

GERALD. Is Humphry Jones to be trusted? (*Little pause.*) Tommy?

TOMMY (*looks at* GERALD). No.

GERALD. You didn't take it to him then?

TOMMY. No, Edie's wrong about that, I took it to him, and I walked about for two hours while he read it, it was very kind of him, you know, on the spot he read it, and then I went back and he told me he thought it wasn't very interesting, straightforwardly and honestly, like a good friend should. So he's a good friend, you see. I've got a friend in Humphry Jones. He'll always turn me down on the spot.

GERALD. But it doesn't matter what Humphry Jones thinks, does it? *You've* still got confidence, haven't you? *You* still like it, don't you?

TOMMY (*after a pause*). No. I think it stinks, you know.

GERALD. So what will you do, Tommy?

Hold on *his face, staring at* TOMMY.

31. Interior. Edith's Study. Day. Come in on *her pen-nib, poised above the page. Then it stabs down, begins to write.*

EDITH (*voice over*). Positively sexual in its execution. (*Repeats.*) And although cerebral in its planning was becoming positively sexual in its execution. She had felt the same sensation when completing her General Paper for her Oxford Scholarship. She was in control, the prize was hers. In the very exactness with which she organized and made lucid her originality there was a respect for convention that could have been interpreted as contempt. So poor Simon's career as her husband was about to be brought to a neat finish, with, of course, a respect for the conventions that marked her contempt for him. Under these circumstances it would have been delightful to make love to him for a last time. She would see if it could could be arranged. The method of dispatch was so orderly, surely a bravura flourish could be permitted. She —

She is interrupted by the roar of a motor-cycle from outside. She turns to the window, looks out.

32. Exterior. Garden. EDITH's point of view *from window:* GERALD, *in his gauntlets, helmet and gloves, is starting the motor-bike, while* TOMMY *in his ludicrous overcoat, is getting into the side-car. The motor-bicycle roars off, up the path.*

33. Interior. Edith's Study. Day. EDITH *smiles contemptuously, returns to her exercise book, dips in her pen.*

EDITH (*voice over continued*). — now saw her mercilessness as a quality of mind —

34. Interior. A Wimpy Bar in a small town. Day. GERALD *and* TOMMY *are seated at a table.*

GERALD. Has it occurred to you that if she hadn't met us when she did, she'd never have written a word. Not a word. Except possibly for a few academic reviews in academic journals. She didn't aspire to creation. She had a first from Oxford and a great gift for thinking dully about dull books. She only took up novels because I was finishing mine and you were in the middle of thinking about beginning yours. If I'd been a weight lifter, she'd have gone in for that.

TOMMY. In the end, she'd have lifted heavier weights.

A WAITRESS puts a coffee in front of GERALD, a Wimpy, a piece of cake and a coffee in front of TOMMY.

GERALD. It took me two years to write my novel, Tommy. Do you remember?

TOMMY, *who is raising the hamburger to his mouth, nods.*

It was gestured at, at the bottom of long reviews on other novels.

TOMMY. I remember.

GERALD. And in three years, she's written four novels —

TOMMY (*his mouth full*). Five almost.

GERALD. And she gets whole reviews to herself, with a photograph inset that was taken when she was twelve. She gets interviewed on average once every three months, with sometimes a reference to myself in the text, or a picture of me striking a husband's pose to the left of her elbow, or with an ear and half an eye showing behind Giles' face. But that's not it, no, that's not it. What it is, is that she sits there in her chaste little cell over her bloody exercise books imitating a schoolgirl imitating a nun, and she still doesn't know how to write a novel. She has a special little gland that other people haven't got, that functions away glandularly, and it makes her richer and richer and more and more famous, and that's not it, either, no, that's not it, it's not even the sum of the injustices of her victories and successes, it is simply that she's killing me. Killing me, yes, that's it.

TOMMY. Killing you?

GERALD. Oh, I don't mean that she's ending our marriage. She's doing that. You today, me tomorrow. Your departure is the means to my end. I mean, she's making me dead.

TOMMY. You hate her then?

GERALD. I'm in love with her. You know, the way one might be with a schoolgirl or a nun, Aren't you?

TOMMY. What? In love — ?

GERALD. Oh come on Tommy. You've *always* been in love with her. I've only just started.

TOMMY *shakes his head.*

Why, you've slept with her, haven't you?

As TOMMY *stares at him, transfixed.*

That year when we were living together. All three of us. Didn't you sleep with her?

TOMMY. Look Gerald, I don't know what you're talking about.

GERALD. Didn't you fancy her, then?

TOMMY (*laughs*). Well of course, that's a different question, isn't it?

GERALD. No it isn't. Everyone was sleeping with everyone. I took it for granted you did with her.

TOMMY. Why didn't you ask me before, then, if you've thought that?

GERALD. I wanted to preserve the proprieties. It doesn't matter any more. So you can tell me. (*Smiling.*) How often did you sleep with my wife?

TOMMY (*laughs*). Well you know, I can't remember. You know, Gerrie —?

GERALD. You do remember, Tommy. Was it once — (*Holds up a finger.*) twice — (*Holds up two fingers.*)

TOMMY *holds up two fingers.*
GERALD *continues to hold up two fingers also.*
They sit staring at each other, holding up two fingers.
Then GERALD *smiles.*

Did you enjoy it?

TOMMY (*shrugs*). Well no, (*lowering his fingers*) it wasn't very successful, it was you she wanted, see.

GERALD. I'm sorry to hear that.

GERALD *begins to laugh.*
TOMMY *also laughs.*
GERALD *draws* TOMMY's *cake to himself, and while he is talking, covers it with various condiments, pepper, salt, mustard, tomato sauce etc.*

Sometimes when you're walking along a street you see a schoolgirl with her satchel, her legs they go down very vulnerable, almost pitiful, into their socks and shoes. Do you know what I mean?

TOMMY *is staring in horror at the cake.*

And one in a hundred has a face, exquisite, sealed off, and you put out of your mind what you know goes through theirs, and you feel it inside you, caught between cherishing and despoiling. (*Little pause.*) The desire to rape nuns is, of course, conventional fantasy. I won't bore you with it. Here — you've had my cake. Now eat yours.

GERALD *pushes the cake at* TOMMY.

TOMMY. Like hell I will, boyo.

GERALD. It's the price you have to pay, Tommy. If you're to inherit my mantle.

TOMMY *shakes his head laughing uncertainly, and then stares down at the cake, back at* GERALD, *and* on his face:

35. Interior. Edith's Study. Day. *Register the sound of her laughing quietly, over the last shot of* GERALD.
EDITH *writing.*

36. Exterior. Garden. MRS MERCHANT *and* GILES *approach up the path.*

37. Interior. Edith's Study. Day. EDITH *writing.*

EDITH (*voice over*). And so he departed, for the last time, from their bedroom, with his tail between and not metaphorically, his legs. With his clothes bundled in his arms and his face bulging with unconsummated aggression, he was not a particularly dignified spectacle. But he had pathos, of a kind that Mathilda knew —

She turns, looks out of the window.

38. Exterior. Garden. EDITH's point of view, GILES *and* MRS MERCHANT *now in the very middle of the path.*

39. Interior. Edith's Study. Day.

EDITH (*voice over*). – in the solitary (*writing quickly*) but by no
means lonely years to come. She– she –

EDITH *stops, smiles at the page, then screws the top on to her
pen, closes the ink-well, blots the page, closes the exercise book,
stands up, stares, smiling, out of the window.*

40. Exterior. Garden. Day. *From* EDITH's point of view. MRS
MERCHANT *lifts* GILES *out of the pram.*

41. Exterior. Country Road. Day. *The motor-bicycle is roaring
at great speed along the road.*
Cut from GERALD's *face, impassive behind goggles, etc, to*
TOMMY's *eyes staring in fright.*
TOMMY *attempts to attract* GERALD's *attention, the motor-
bicycle roars on,* past the camera, see it from behind, *suddenly
slowing and then stopping.*
TOMMY *scrambles out of the side-car and runs, clutching his
stomach, to the bushes.*

42. Exterior. The Garden. Day. EDITH *is pushing* GILES *in the
pram slowly up the path, towards* MRS MERCHANT.

43. The Road. Day. *The motor-bike roaring along the road,* cut
from GERALD's *face, to* TOMMY's, *crumpled in misery.*

44. The Garden. Day. EDITH, MRS MERCHANT, GILES, *in the
middle of the path as before.*
*Sound over of the motor-bike and as they look up, the motor-
bike is roaring towards them, and* cut to *their reactions,* then to
TOMMY's *face, stiff with horror.* Then GERALD's,
indecipherable behind the goggles, etc.

45. Interior. Living Room. Day. Come in directly on GERALD's
face, now without goggles, helmet, etc. He is sitting impassively.
Then take in TOMMY, *sitting on the sofa, clearly shaken.*

The door opens, MRS MERCHANT *comes out, walks past*
GERALD, *stiff faced.*
GERALD *follows her with his eyes, then looks towards the door,*
as EDITH *comes out, closing it behind her.*
Baby noise off from GILES.

EDITH. You nearly killed us all. Do you realise that?

GERALD. It *was* a close thing, wasn't it? Old Tommy would have
thrown up his gâteau vinaigrette if he hadn't already thrown it up.

EDITH. Are you being defiant, or are you actually a little mad?

GERALD. A little mad actually. (*He gets up and goes to the door.*)
You've got a lunatic on your hands. I give you warning. (*He*
smiles, goes out.)

TOMMY (*to* EDITH, *who is staring after* GERALD). Edie . . . .
um, you know, he's, well —

EDITH *turns, looks at him.*

It's — it's — look Edie, he isn't well, there's something wrong
with him, I don't mean he tried to run you over or anything
like that, see, but he might do something desperate, if you ask
me.

EDITH. And if I ask you, what would you suggest?

TOMMY. You shouldn't be alone together, not just now, Edith.

EDITH. Tommy, I asked you to go. Are you going to, please.

TOMMY. He hates you, you know.

EDITH. Of course he does. Why should he make an exception of
me. He almost certainly hates you too.

EDITH *goes out.* TOMMY *stands for a moment, on his face an*
expression of rage.

46. Interior. Gerald's Study. Day. GERALD *is lying on the camp*
bed, smoking a cheroot.
TOMMY *comes in.*

TOMMY. I'll stay if you tell me to . . .

GERALD (*looks at him*). *Tell* you to?

TOMMY. Yes.

GERALD. Well, I won't. I'd prefer you gone. I need you somewhere else, Tommy.

TOMMY, *after a moment, goes to his suitcase under the camp bed, drags it out, begins to shut it.*

Could I have my shirts back, please.

TOMMY. I've soiled them.

GERALD. The soil may belong to you, the shirts belong to me.

TOMMY *takes out the shirts, puts them on the bed, closes the suitcase.*

How romantic, to travel light. You don't mind if I don't take you to the station after all.

TOMMY (*looks at him, after a pause*). Will there be a train?

GERALD. At the station? Well, if you don't find one there, you won't find one anywhere.

TOMMY (*suddenly firm*). Could I have my coat please.

GERALD. It's behind you.

TOMMY. The one I inherited.

GERALD. Inherited?

TOMMY. The one I ate that cake for.

GERALD. Oh, you misunderstood me. I was speaking poetically.

TOMMY (*desperately*). What is it you want me to do, then? What?

GERALD. Go.

TOMMY *turns, goes out of the door.*

47. Interior. Edith's Study. Day. EDITH *is standing at the window looking out, and* from her point of view, *through the window, sees* TOMMY *plodding up the path.*

48. Exterior. Garden. Day. From EDITH's point of view, TOMMY *plodding up the path. He is carrying his suitcase, and wearing his ludicrous overcoat.*

49. Interior. Edith's Study. Day. *For a moment* EDITH *looks uncertain, as if perhaps on the verge of calling out to* TOMMY.

50. Exterior. Garden. Day. *There is the roar of the motor-bike and* GERALD *comes into view, stops beside* TOMMY, *talks to him.* TOMMY *gets into the side-car.*

51. Interior. Edith's Study. Day. EDITH *turns away to her desk. She sits down at it, stares ahead for a moment, then unscrews the top of her fountain pen, opens the exercise book, then sits staring at the page. On her face.*

52. Interior. The bedroom. Night. EDITH *is lying in bed reading 'Persuasion.' Beisde her the baby-alarm is on. The sound of* GILES's *breathing.* Hold on this, *then the roar of the motor-bike, and immediately, from the baby-alarm,* GILES's *cry.* EDITH *starts, sits still, then makes as if to get up. The crying stops.*
She gets back into bed, sits tensely.
A few snuffling noises from the box, then silence.
Sound of a door opening and closing, footsteps.
GERALD *comes in, closes the door behind him. On his face is an expression so impassive that it is sinister. He begins to get undressed.*

EDITH. I think you'd better sleep in the study. As it's free now.

GERALD. No, I'll sleep with you tonight. It'll be the last time.

EDITH. Yes.

> *There is a silence as* GERALD *goes on undressing.* Keep on EDITH's *face, watching him. It is very composed, but a hint of excitement.*

GERALD. By the way, Tommy informs me you've slept with him.

EDITH. Really?

GERALD. You did then?

EDITH. Tommy is a liar. I've never gone in for adultery.

GERALD. I wasn't asking after your religious habits. I was indirectly asking whether you and Tommy had ever copulated with each other.

EDITH. Are you hoping he did? Do you think that jealousy is less demeaning than envy?

> *As* GERALD *gets into bed.*

I'd be grateful if you'd wash. You're dirty.

GERALD *lies staring up at the ceiling.*
EDITH *picks up 'Persuasion'.*

GERALD. There is, I suppose, the faint possibility that Giles isn't mine?

EDITH. Would it make any difference if he weren't?

GERALD (*reaches past her, turns off baby-alarm*). I'd like to think he'd disgust me just as much if I were sure he were.

EDITH. You are literally hateful. Full of hate. *Did* you try to harm him this afternoon?

GERALD *suddenly rolls over, looks down at her, then takes the book from her hand, and drops it over the edge of the bed.*
EDITH *laughs.*
GERALD *puts a hand on her breast.*

EDITH (*ironically*). Oh dear.

GERALD *slaps her.*

You don't have to do that. I'm yours.

GERALD *stares at her blankly, and* EDITH *smiles.*
He begins to make love to her. As he does so, EDITH's *hand comes out, turns on the baby-alarm. Her hand withdraws but stay on the baby-alarm. A few small cries come from it, and cries from* EDITH, *then on a full cry from* EDITH, *cut to:* EDITH's *face, she is flushed and smiling. A small, triumphant smile. Then take in* GERALD *beside her. He is lying, staring up.*

(*She turns towards him.*) Oh dear. (*Pause.*) I'm sorry.

GERALD *goes on staring up. Then suddenly he begins to cry.*
EDITH *stares at him, her smile becoming suddenly uncertain.*

Gerrie — (*whispered*) Gerrie —

And aghast she puts her hand to his head, stares into his face. He is still crying.

Gerrie —

He stares at her pathetically.
He rolls away, gets out of bed, picks up his clothes, goes to the door, turns, stares at her. On his face, an expression of dreadful malevolence. He goes out.
EDITH *stares after him, makes as if to follow him, then lies*

back, hold on *her face, suggesting time passing. Her expression
tense.*
Then the roar of the motor-bike, the sound fading way.

A pause.

(*Her voice slightly shaky.*) That's that, then. (*Little pause.*)
Consummatum est. (*She laughs, still shakily.*)

53. Interior. Gerald's Study. Day. Hold on *the room, in its
slovenliness. Then* EDITH *comes on camera. Purposefully, almost
violently, she rips the covers off the camp bed. Then* a series of
shots, montage, *of her cleaning out and cleaning up the room,
with a kind of fanatical intensity,* culminating with two last
shots, sustained longer than the others, *of her wrapping up*
GERALD's *manuscripts in brown paper, tying them into a
parcel, then putting the hood over the typewriter.*
Move back to *the door, where* EDITH *stands when she has
finished.* Take in *the room, bare and as if purged. She turns, goes
out.*

54. Interior. Bathroom sink. Day. On EDITH's *hands, as they are
briskly washing themselves,* EDITH's *face in the mirror as she
combs her hair.*

55. Interior. Edith's Study. Day. *She goes to the window, stands
for a second, then turns to her desk, picks up the exercise books
to the left, the ones filled, holds them almost devotionally, smiles.
She puts them down, sits down, takes out her pen, opens the ink-
well then turns the exercise book open. The page is blank. She
frowns, turns back a page. Also blank. She picks the exercise
book up, riffles through it, blank. In horror she picks up the
filled exercise books, riffles through them. On the last page of the
last exercise book, scrawled in large letters: 'Go back to page one.'*

56. Interior. The kitchen. Day. EDITH *is sitting at the table,
staring ahead.*
*Her face is over-composed, as if against panic. She gets up, goes
to the phone, opens the address book beside it, begins to dial. Then*
cut to *shots of her finger on different telephone numbers, dialing*

with the other finger, to suggest numerous phone calls being made, then cut to:
EDITH *sitting at the table again. There is the sound of a motor-car outside, a honk.*
She gets up, picks up a coat and handbag, already arranged on a chair, goes to the back door, opens it. And finds herself facing MRS MERCHANT, GILES *in her arms.*
EDITH *blinks in a shock of recognition.*

EDITH. Um, um — I've got to go to London on — um, something urgent. Could you do Giles until, I um — if I'm late? It's terribly urgent.

MRS MERCHANT. Of course, it's nothing serious is it?

EDITH. Yes. (*Makes to go.*)

MRS MERCHANT. I'll tell Mr Dunlop you've gone.

EDITH. Oh, he won't be — yes, if he comes, tell him he must wait for me. He must. All right?

She looks at GILES, *kisses him as if remembering, goes out.*

57. Exterior. Garden. Day. Shot of EDITH, *from* MRS MERCHANT's point of view, *getting into a taxi.*

58. Interior. David's Office. Day. Come in on EDITH's *face, seen from* DAVID's point of view. *She looks exhausted.*

EDITH. Credit where it's due. It's effectively humiliating. I spent the morning on the telephone to people I haven't seen for months, for years. Asking them if they'd seen my husband. They hadn't, of course. But they found the question interesting. One or two hinted that I'd dropped them with my success. I longed to say that I'd been merciful. If I'd dropped them when I'd been a failure they'd have had to attribute some fault to themselves. This way I gave them the opportunity to blame me. The afternoon I spent in familiar half-forgotten pubs, not knowing whose eyes to dodge and whose to catch. None of them looked as if they could have belonged to my past, but they might all have belonged to *his*. I don't know. I can't remember. How could I? (*Little pause.*) I should have thought. I should have *thought*. But it was the one unthinkable thing. (*Little pause.*) But he thought of it. Why didn't I? I should

have slept with them under my pillow, had them chained to
my wrist, hidden them under the floor-boards, until he'd
gone. (*Little pause.*) But I've worked out this much. He
wouldn't have put the blank ones there if he'd decided to
(*with an effort*) destroy the other ones. He'd have left torn
pages, or embers, or nothing. He *must* be going to use them —
as hostages, so to speak. (*She smiles.*) What shall I do? (*Lips
tremble.*) David?

She attempts a smile. On her face.

59. Exterior. Drive. Day. *Taxi coming towards the drive.* But
carry on shot of EDITH's face from previous scene, and then cut
to:

60. Interior. Kitchen window. Day. MRS MERCHANT's *face
staring out, desperately worried.*

61. Exterior. Garden. MRS MERCHANT's point of view. *A
taxi draws up, beside a car.*
EDITH *gets out, paying the taxi-driver hastily, looks at the car,
begins to run towards the house.*
MRS MERCHANT *hurries to the door, opens it, and see her face
worried, from* EDITH's point of view.

MRS MERCHANT. I don't know what's wrong, Dr Slocum's
with him now.

EDITH *runs past her.*

62. Interior. Giles's Room. Day. *Terrible cries coming from*
GILES. DR SLOCUM *is straightening up from the cot,
stethoscope dangling from his ears. He turns, stares at* EDITH,
his face severe.
EDITH *stares back at him, panic stricken.*
MRS MERCHANT *comes in behind her.*

EDITH. Oh God, what's the matter.

DR SLOCUM. I've not the slightest idea. His lungs are in
excellent shape, at least.

EDITH (*confused, shouting*). What?

She goes to the cot, looks down at GILES. *She picks him up.*
GILES *begins to calm down.*

DR SLOCUM. But whatever it was, I can't believe it was worth
calling me out for. We've got the summer 'flu epidemic on our
hands, you know.

EDITH. Called — who called?

She looks accusingly at MRS MERCHANT.

MRS MERCHANT (*indignantly*). I didn't —

DR SLOCUM. The call was from your husband. (*Packing his bag.*)
He said your child needed attention. (*Straightening, and on his
face, cut to:*)

63. Interior. Bedroom. Night. EDITH *is in bed, reading. The book
held up to her face. She lowers the book. She is crying, silently.
She wipes her eyes with the sheets, lies still for a moment. Then
turns out the light, there is a pause.*
*The light comes on again. She lies staring ahead, as if trying to
remember something, then suddenly turns her head to the baby-
alarm which is silent. She stares at it in panic, then grabs it, turns
up the sound. Still nothing. She makes to get out of bed,
suddenly remembers the on-off switch. Fumblingly she checks it,
turns it to on. The sound of* GILES *breathing. She turns the light
on. Picks up the book, resolutely, begins to read.*

EDITH. The sod! The hateful sod!

Fade into a shot of EDITH *asleep, the light on, the book open
beside her.*
*It is still night. There is over, the distant noise of the motor-
bicycle, very muted, being driven at the lowest possible throttle.
Her eyes flicker open. She stares ahead, then sits up as the
noise goes on, slightly louder.*
*The noise stops. Cut to her face, listening, waiting. Sounds of
a key in the lock, a door opening, closing quietly, footsteps,
other doors opening and closing. Then silence.* EDITH *gets up,
goes to the bedroom door, opens it. Follow her through to:*

64. Interior. Various Rooms. Night. GERALD's *study. On to her
own study, the door is open. She goes to it.*

65. Interior. Edith's Study. Night. *What appears to be* GERALD's *back — it is, in fact,* TOMMY, *in* GERALD's *coat. His head is bent low as he fumbles inside* EDITH's *desk. Cut to her face, resolute as she walks quickly and softly over, puts her hand on his arm.* TOMMY *jumps, looks up.*
EDITH *stares into his face, see it full in camera, from her point of view, then back to* EDITH.

EDITH. What do you want?

TOMMY. Oh, I'm sorry Edie (*nervously*) I — I — was just — well, see the thing is Gerald asked me to get something for him.

EDITH. He's got them all. There aren't any more.

TOMMY. What? Sleeping pills? He says he hasn't, Edith, no look.

He holds a bottle out in the palm of his hand.

He said you kept an extra bottle in your desk —

EDITH. You came here for that?

TOMMY (*shrugs*). Well, he asked me to come and get them, Edie. He said he needed them.

EDITH (*after a pause*). What are you doing in his coat?

TOMMY. Well, he gave it to me in the end, you see. I won it in one of our bets. It was a cake I had to eat, he —

EDITH. Where is he Tommy? Where is he?

TOMMY. Well, I promised him I wouldn't say. He said you'd ask, he made me promise, Edie.

EDITH. He's got my exercise books, you know. My novel. I want them back.

TOMMY. Of course you do. Of course.

EDITH. He's not in London then?

TOMMY. No.

EDITH. Has it occurred to you that he's ill.

TOMMY looks at her as if wavering.
EDITH goes to him, clutches his arm.

Tommy, take me to him. (*Little pause.*) Please.

TOMMY looks at her. She is pleading, but there is something deliberately sexual in her appeal.

Please? (*Wonderingly.*) Don't tell me anything. Just take me to him. You didn't promise him you wouldn't do that, did you?

TOMMY. No. (*Little pause.*) Do you mean now?

EDITH (*gently*). Please, Tommy.

TOMMY (*after a pause*). But what about Giles, you couldn't leave him all by himself then, could you?

EDITH, *as if realising, shakes her head.*

EDITH. I'd — I'd — (*Stops.*) Well then, ask him to give me a ring, will you please.

TOMMY. Yes. Yes, I'll do that.

He hesitates, then takes EDITH in his arms, kisses her gently on the mouth, then stands hesitant.

I'll tell him to give you a ring then.

He goes out. Keep on *the door, sound of doors opening, then* EDITH *goes to the hall, and through to:*

66. Interior. The kitchen. Night. EDITH *goes to the window, looks out.*

67. The Garden. Night. *There is a figure on the seat of the motor-bicycle, in crash-helmet and goggles, indistinct. She stares towards it, through the window, assuming that it is* TOMMY.
The figure raises an arm, in salute, then TOMMY *appears, in goggles and helmet, climbs into the side-car. All this from* EDITH's *point of view.*

68. Interior. The kitchen. Night. EDITH *stares at the motor-bike, then realizing, runs to the kitchen door.*

69. The Garden. Night. EDITH *opens kitchen door, as* GERALD, *on the seat, kicks the motor-bike into life, it cruises up the drive.* Cut to EDITH's *face, and from that* cut to:

70. Interior. Edith's Study. Morning. EDITH *is sitting at the desk, she stares blankly ahead, then takes a fresh exercise book, opens* *it. She picks up her fountain pen, lifts the lid of the ink-well. Dips the pen in. Her pen hovers. She writes:*

EDITH (*voice over*). Mathilda felt that — Mathilda felt that she — Mathilda felt — Mathilda — Mathilda —

Having stopped writing, she turns her head, looks out of the window, and, from her point of view, cut to:

71. The Garden. Day. Shot of MRS MERCHANT, *with* GILES *in the pram, just leaving the house.*

72. Interior. Edith's Study. Day. EDITH *suddenly screws the top back on her pen, snaps the ink-well shut, very quickly hurries out of the room.*

73. The Garden. Day. Shot of MRS MERCHANT *and* GILES *as if through the study window, as* EDITH *runs up to her, takes over the pram, begins to push it.*
MRS MERCHANT *walks beside her, as, over, the sound of the telephone ringing.*
EDITH *stops. Turns around, runs back to the house, all this seen as through the study window, then* cut to:

74. Interior. Kitchen. Day. EDITH *hurrying to the telephone, picks it up a fraction after it stops ringing. The dialling tone is audible. She stands holding it, then puts it down. She stands looking at it, then goes back to the open kitchen door.*

75. Day. *From* EDITH's *point of view at the kitchen door,* MRS MERCHANT *and* GILES, *waiting.*

EDITH (*shouting*). I shan't be coming. You go on.

MRS MERCHANT *turns, goes down the path.*
EDITH *watches, then turns, goes back in, shuts the door.*

76. Interior, Kitchen. Day. EDITH *goes to the stove, puts on the kettle, and* cut to:

EDITH *sitting at the table, drinking a cup of tea. The telephone rings. She leaps up, goes over to it, picks it up.*

EDITH. Hello. Hello.

There is a click of the receiver being replaced at the other end. She puts the telephone down, goes back to the table. Sits. The telephone rings again. She leaps up, it stops ringing. She stares at it.
She sits down, almost gingerly. It rings. She gets up. It stops ringing. She remains poised between sitting and standing, staring at the telephone, and cut to:

77. Interior. Giles's bedroom. Day. Come in on GILES, *nappy off, then* come in on MRS MERCHANT, *dropping the dirty nappy into a bucket. She smiles down at GILES and cut to:*
EDITH *at the door, comes in, stares down at GILES.*

EDITH. Hello darling.

MRS MERCHANT. I was just going to do his rash.

EDITH. Were you? I'll do it.

As MRS MERCHANT opens the jar of ointment, EDITH dips her finger into it, takes sone ointment out on the end of her finger, when the telephone rings.
MRS MERCHANT *turns towards the door, as if to answer the telephone.*

I'll get it.

She pushes past MRS MERCHANT, handing her GILES, and leaves the room.
MRS MERCHANT *looks at GILES, then puts her finger into the jar, as the telephone stops ringing. There is a short pause.*
EDITH *reappears.*
MRS MERCHANT, *not seeing her, is about to apply the cream.*

(*With a tight smile.*) I said I'd do it.

She is still holding her fingers ahead of her. On them, Baby-cream.
MRS MERCHANT *steps aside, offended.*
EDITH *advances towards GILES, as the telephone rings.*
EDITH *stiffens, then making an immense effort, goes on dabbing the cream.*
The telephone goes on ringing. She goes on dabbing the cream,

finishes, wipes her fingers. The telephone is still ringing. She turns to MRS MERCHANT.

Would you do his nappy, please.

She walks out of the room, and cut to:

78. Interior The Kitchen. Day. EDITH *walks steadily towards the telephone, picks it up. She waits a second, as if expecting a click. There is a pause.*

EDITH. Hello. (*There is a silence.*) Hello. Giles?

GERALD. Gerald.

EDITH (*smiles very slightly*). Gerald. Yes.

GERALD. You asked me to give you a ring.

EDITH. Yes. (*Ironically.*) Thank you.

GERALD. I've given you several. I shan't be giving you any more.

Click, as he hangs up.
EDITH *stands there, holding the receiver, then bangs it down, then picks it up and bangs it down several times, in a fury. Stops, begins to walk away.*

The telephone rings. EDITH *turns, stares at it, then picks it up.*

Edith? Gerald here. Hello again! Look old girl — it occurred to me you might want something. Is there anything?

EDITH (*controlling herself*). You know what I want. (*There is a silence.*) Don't you?

GERALD (*after a pause*). Me?

EDITH. I want my novel back. (*Long pause.*) Are you there?

GERALD. Yes — yes, I'm here. Is there anything else you want?

EDITH. I'd like to talk to you. Properly.

GERALD. Would you like to see my room? Where I'm living, and how I've settled down?

EDITH. Yes. (*Quickly.*) Where is it?

GERALD. Oh, better to pick you up, I think. If you don't mind riding in the old side-car, that is?

EDITH. No. That'll be all right.

GERALD. Say in an hour.

EDITH. Yes. Yes. In an hour.

GERALD. In an hour.

Click as he puts the telephone down.

EDITH *replaces the telephone, turns, sees* MRS MERCHANT *standing before her, holding* GILES. *Looks at her, looks at* GILES, *then, as if realising.*

EDITH. Oh. Mrs Merchant. Um, would you mind terribly holding the, um . . .

Cut to:

79. Interior. Kitchen. Day. MRS MERCHANT, *her face staring out of the window.*

80. The Garden. Day. From MRS MERCHANT's point of view. *At kitchen window see* EDITH *walking down the path to the motorbike. There is a man sitting on it in* GERALD's *coat goggles, etc.* EDITH *says something to him,* cut to:

TOMMY. All I know, Edie, is he told me to bring you. Isn't that all right?

EDITH, *after a pause, gets into the side-car, it roars off. And* cut back to:

81. Interior. Kitchen. Day. MRS MERCHANT *at the window, turning away. And* cut to:

82. Exterior. The Hotel. Day. *The motor-bike pulling up before a large shabby house converted into a shabby private hotel.* TOMMY *gets off.* EDITH *gets out,* TOMMY *takes* EDITH's *arm, they walk up the steps to the front door, and* cut to:

83. Interior. The Hotel. Day. *They go up grubby stairs, passing a lounge-type room. From which comes the noise of a television set. Then up more stairs past various doors with numbers half-erased. They reach the last two doors, next to each other.*

TOMMY. This is his, Edie.

EDITH. I think I'd better do this alone, if you don't mind.

TOMMY. Of course, Edie.

He turns, to go to the other room, stops as EDITH *makes to knock.*

Look, I'll be in here if you need me. See.

EDITH *looks at him, then turns to* GERALD's *door, knocks. There is no reply.* EDITH *knocks again, then turns the handle. The door opens. She goes in. The light is on. The bed is unmade. There are clothes spilled everywhere, and a general sense of muddle and squalor. Propped against the mirror there is a note, on which is written: 'This is my room'.*
EDITH *reads the note, turns, looks around. Makes as if to go out, then turns, goes to the chest of drawers, cupboard, bed, each one in turn, hunts rapidly through them, then stops, stares around, and* cut to:
TOMMY's *room. It is in the same condition as* GERALD's. TOMMY *is sitting in an arm-chair.* Come in on *his face, looking towards the door, then* cut to:

EDITH (*at the door*). He's not there. (*Little pause.*) Of course.

TOMMY. Oh.

He gets to his feet, as if about to go and look.

EDITH. He's not there. He never intended to be. Where is he?

TOMMY. I don't know. (*Little pause.*) Edie, I don't know. Look, he said I was to pick you up and take you to his room, seeing as you wanted to see it, that was all, Edie.

EDITH (*advances towards him*). You're lying. You're lying. (*Stands in front of him.*) All the money you've borrowed and never mentioned again — all the food you've guzzled — the drink you've got drunk on to give yourself the courage to bore and insult my friends — who do you think buys him those shirts you make dirty, his coat — that coat — *I* gave it to him, my books gave it to him, to you — you owe me, you owe me. (*Punching at his chest.*) Now you tell me, tell me, tell me!

Her voice is rising hysterically, and cut to:
The Hall, before the front door.
TOMMY *holds the door open for* EDITH. *She steps out, he follows, his hand on her arm. He closes the door, and from the doorstep, their point of view,* cut to:

84. Exterior. Hotel. Day. GERALD *in* TOMMY's *coat, on the motor-bicycle, driving away.*
TOMMY *and* EDITH *stand staring after him, and* cut to:

85. Exterior. The drive. Day. Come in on MRS MERCHANT, medium shot, *coming up the drive. Her walk — seen from in front is jerky, odd.* Hold, then cut to:

86. Interior. Taxi. Day. EDITH *is sitting forward, staring towards* MRS MERCHANT *who is walking towards them, she taps on the glass, stops the taxi. She opens the window and leans out of it.*
Close-up *of* MRS MERCHANT's *face, seen from* EDITH's point of view.
Tears are streaming down her cheeks. She makes to open her mouth, closes it, clearly very distraught. But there is something sinister in the effect.
EDITH *gets out, starts after her, clutches her arm.*
MRS MERCHANT *turns, says something,* EDITH *says something then turns, runs towards the house.*
TOMMY *has got out of the taxi, and is following slowly. He stops, turns back to the taxi.*

87. Interior. Kitchen. Day. EDITH *flings open the door* shot from inside the kitchen then a brisk montage *as she runs through the house, comes to* GILES's *room, goes in.* GILES *is asleep.*
EDITH *turns, comes out, walks back to the kitchen.*
TOMMY *is standing just inside the door.*

EDITH. He's here somewhere.

TOMMY. Is he?

EDITH. He must have been. He's just sacked Mrs Merchant.

She goes to the door, looks out.

88. Exterior. Garden. Day. *From* EDITH's *point of view at kitchen door, see taxi still there. There is a short, intense silence, then* GERALD's *motor-bike starts up (not seen) and roars around the house into sight, up the drive, past the taxi and away. There is a pause.*

89. Interior. Kitchen. Day. EDITH *turns, looks at* TOMMY.

TOMMY (*licks his lips*). I haven't got any money, Edith.

EDITH. What?

TOMMY. For the taxi. To get me back to Guildford, see.

   EDITH *starts to laugh, stops, opens her handbag, fumbles in it. Then looks at* TOMMY.

EDITH. You've got to make him come here and talk to me.

   She takes a five-pound note out of her wallet, hands it to him.

   Will you?

   TOMMY *looks at the money, then at* EDITH.

TOMMY. This is a fiver, did you know, Edie?

EDITH (*after a slight pause*). I haven't got anything smaller. That's all I have.

   TOMMY *puts his hand into his pocket.*

TOMMY. Oh look, I've got a pound. I won't need this after all.

   He hands it back to EDITH.

   Thanks.

EDITH. Please, Tommy.

   Cut to *her face.*

   Please.

90. Interior. Edith's Bedroom. Night. EDITH *is asleep, 'Persuasion' lying open beside her. The lamp is on the floor, lamp-shade tilted, to soften the light. The baby-alarm is on. Gentle sounds of* GILES *breathing. Keep on* EDITH's *face. She sits up suddenly, stares around. Gets up, walks to the door. There should be something almost somnambulistic in her movements.*

91. Interior. Living room. Night. *She goes down the hall, opens the door to the living-room. Stands blinking.*
Then cut to GERALD *sitting in a chair, in* TOMMY's *coat, facing her.*

Cut back to EDITH.

GERALD (*smiling, voice gentle*). I've come, you see.

EDITH. Yes. (*Quietly.*) Just a minute. I'm not properly awake. I've got to be awake to say the right words, haven't I? (*She smiles, goes out.*)

92. Interior. Bathroom. Night. Cut to EDITH *washing her face under the cold tap.*

93. Interior. Living room. Night. Then cut to EDITH, *drops of water still on her face, coming back to the sitting room. It is empty. She stares around as:*
GERALD *comes out of* GILES's *room, closing the door quietly.*

GERALD. It's all right, I haven't gone. (*He sits down.*)

EDITH. You've grown so expert in your games. (*Smiling, gentle.*) They're very literary. Literal, in fact. That's why I have to get the right words.

She is walking slowly towards him, then crouches down at his feet, takes his hand.

There. I've got you.

GERALD *puts his hand on hers.*

GERALD. I didn't realise you wanted me.

EDITH. Please Gerrie, could I have it back? Please.

She smiles up at him.

GERALD (*carefully*). Would you say you wanted it more than anything?

EDITH. Is that what you've been proving to me? I knew it already. I've known it since I started writing — since about the third paragraph of my first novel. It's the only thing nobody would ever have to prove to me. I'm not ashamed, either. I'm not ashamed.

GERALD. And what would become of me, if I gave it back? How would I sustain your interest? You've tried to catch my every move, these last few days.

EDITH. You could come here again, if you wanted. For as long as you wanted. And Tommy too.

GERALD. Would you love us?

EDITH (*after a pause*). I would do my best.

GERALD. I could make love to you?

EDITH (*with a slight, malicious smile*). You could do your best.

GERALD. Ah! (*He smiles. Touches the side of her cheek.*)
And if it's too late? If I haven't got the exercise books any more?

EDITH *thinks, then very carefully.*

EDITH. I think I'd like to see you die.

GERALD (*nods*). Then it's too late for me. I haven't got them any more.

EDITH *stares up at him, frozen. Then slowly gets up, walks to a chair opposite, sits down, looks at* GERALD. *She tries to smile.*

EDITH. What did you do with them?

GERALD (*shakes his head*). It doesn't matter any more. Not to me. (*He puts his hand into his pocket.*) Did you find the right words, do you think?

EDITH's *mouth is trembling, but her voice is controlled, as if with a tremendous effort.*

EDITH. I shall start again. And once I've started, what you've done won't mean anything.

GERALD *is holding sleeping pills, not of course registered by* EDITH − *in his cupped hand.*

He begins to pop them into his mouth, as if they were smarties.

GERALD. You'll be able to say of me . . . (*Popping them into his mouth nonchalantly*) . . . that I was literal to the end.

EDITH. Perhaps doing it again is only right. It'll be different, there will be things to add − but above all − you won't be here. What you've done *will* mean something. But to me. Not to you. You're so much waste, got rid of. And there's nothing more you can do to hurt me, you see.

GERALD. I know. That's the appalling thing about you.

EDITH (*smiles*). Would you go now, please. (*Getting up.*)

GERALD. Oh. Aren't you going to stay. I thought you wanted to see me — um, die. (*Modestly*.)

EDITH *stares at him, aghast.*
GERALD *throws the last few sleeping pills into his mouth, swallows them down with a gulp. Then shows her the bottle.*

Isn't that what you wanted?

EDITH (*after a pause*). How many have you taken?

GERALD. Twenty-two.

EDITH. You're a child. A nasty child.

Long pause, she stares at him. GERALD *is staring up at her.*

GERALD. And my games are so literal. But the words *were* yours. Weren't they the right ones, after all?

EDITH (*after a pause*). Do you want me to telephone for a doctor then? If you do, say so.

GERALD. Oh, that's *your* business.

EDITH. I'll do what *you* tell me to do.

GERALD. Then — do whatever you think is best. You have your church, your art, and your education. If the maxims you derive from each should conflict, you will have to choose.

EDITH (*after a pause*). How do you feel?

GERALD. A trifle nervous. But physically tip-top. The system needs about twenty minutes to absorb them. After that it's down-hill all the way. But I believe the decline can be arrested until I go into a coma.

EDITH. In other words, you can reach the telephone unaided.

She turns, goes out.
Cut to GERALD's *face, he smiles, uncertainly. There is a pause.*
EDITH *returns, walks past him, into* GILES's *room. There is the sound of a protest from* GILES, *sleepy.*
She comes out, carrying him. Walks past GERALD, *and out of the room.*
Cut to GERALD's *face. He sits resolutely. Crosses his hands in his lap. Licks his lip. His face twitches slightly. He raises a hand, scratches at his cheek as if he had an itch there. Then lowers his hand, raises it, scratches again, blinks.*

94. Interior. Bedroom. Night. EDITH *is sitting up in bed, staring ahead.*
GILES *is lying beside her, asleep. She picks her watch up from the table, looks at it, puts it down.*
She turns, looks down at GILES *and,* cut to *his face asleep.*
EDITH's *hand, shaking, goes to his hair, touches it and* cut from this to:

95. Interior. Living Room. Night. GERALD's *face, eyes closed, mouth open in a yawn. His hand is resting against his cheek. His eyes blink open. He stares blearily around, heaves himself up, gropes forward, stands swaying, and* cut to:

96. Interior. Bedroom. Night. EDITH *is sitting up, staring ahead with great intensity. She closes her eyes, opens them.*
Suddenly there is a crash, eerily distanced.
Her head jerks in alarm as the room fills with heavy breathing. She looks towards the baby-alarm.
The breathing is coming from it. She jerks her head away, stares ahead. Then reaches out a hand trembling slightly, to the alarm, turns it off. Then she sits with her head sunk on her chest, eyes closed.
Fade out *on this, and* fade up *on* EDITH *lying, her face sideways on the pillow, her thumb in her mouth, staring into* GILES's *face, also sideways on the pillow, thumb in his mouth, asleep. She straightens slowly, turns to the baby-alarm, still sucking on her thumb. She reaches out a hand. Turns on the knob.*
The breathing is now stertorous, rasping. She turns the knob off quickly, blinks and as if coming to herself, swings her legs out of bed. She hurries out of the bedroom and cut to:

97. Interior. Hall. Night. EDITH *is in the hall, and* from her point of view. Cut to *the door to* GERALD's *study. It opens.*
EDITH *is staring at it, making incomprehensible noises of fear.*
TOMMY *is standing there, in* GERALD's *coat, goggles pushed up on his forehead, helmet and gauntlets under his arm.*

TOMMY. I'm cold. (*Slightly whining.*) He told me to wait outside, with the bike, where is he then?

EDITH's *lips move for a second. She gives a ghastly grin.*

EDITH. Asleep.

Cut to:

98. Interior. Giles's Bedroom. Night. Come straight in on
GERALD, *lying on the floor, snoring heavily. The baby-alarm
microphone close to his face.*
Then cut to TOMMY's *face, shocked and bewildered, staring at*
GERALD.

TOMMY. Ohh — Ohh — look now — look — Edie we've got to —
look.

(*Little pause.*)

What are we going to do, then? What are we going to do?

(Cut to EDITH's *face. She is staring at* TOMMY. *Cut to:*)

99. Exterior. The drive. Dawn. *In on* GERALD's *face, in close-up,
in goggles and crash helmet.*
Then draw back *to see him in the side-car, with his head back and
his mouth open, breathing deeply. Then his face is drawn slowly
out of camera and:*
Cut to:
TOMMY *and* GERALD, *on the motor-bicycle and side-car
respectively, pulling quietly down the drive,* from EDITH's point
of view.*watching from the window, then* cut to:
Her face at the window, staring out.

100. Exterior. Field. Day. *A path across a field. The motor-bike
travelling slowly and eerily across it, and from a distance, see the
motor-bicycle stopping.*
TOMMY *pulls* GERALD *out of the side-car, lowers him to the
ground, then* TOMMY *walks away, running, walking, running, and:*
Cut to:

101. Exterior. Mrs Merchant's house. Day. *The gate to the front
door,* MRS MERCHANT *standing before it, arms akimbo.* EDITH,
with the pram.

MRS MERCHANT. I've never been spoken to like that before. Never in my life.

EDITH. He'll never speak to you like that again. I promise.

(*Little pause.*)

He left me — just after he — he'd spoken to you. He said he wouldn't come back.

(*Little pause.*)

We've always had such a good relationship Mrs Merchant.

(*Little pause.*)

Please. We need you, Giles and I. We do need you.

102. Interior. The kitchen. Day. Come in on TOMMY's *hand, raising a cup to his lips, then to his face. He looks desperately tired.* EDITH *sits opposite, watching him.*

TOMMY. Could it be murder, Edie?

EDITH. It was suicide.

TOMMY. But legally? I mean, if the police —?

EDITH. He wanted to kill himself. He wanted to do it in the way that would hurt me most. He was determined to be hateful to the end.

(*Little pause.*)

He had the right to kill himself. I had the right to defend myself from the consequences of his doing it here.

TOMMY. You said yourself he was ill. He needed help —

EDITH *looks at him very coldly.*

EDITH. Well, you didn't give it to him, did you?

TOMMY. No. I gave it to you instead.

EDITH. Why?

TOMMY. You know why, now. Don't you?

EDITH. Are you in love with me?

TOMMY. I've always been, Edie. Always. (*Little pause.*) And did Gerrie ask you about it? About whether we'd ever slept together.

EDITH (*after a pause*). No. Anyway, it was a long time ago.

TOMMY. Still, he asked *me*. I was just wondering –

EDITH. What did you tell him? (*Little pause.*) *Did* you tell him?

TOMMY. Certainly not. No. I told him it was ridiculous.

EDITH. And so it was. It always is. Quite ridiculous. Everything is ridiculous. Gerald's death.

The telephone rings. EDITH and TOMMY stare at each other. She gets up, lifts the telephone from the receiver, staring at TOMMY, then turns away, puts it to her ear.

Hello. (*Little pause.*) Yes, it is. (*Brightly smiling.*)

103. Interior. Hospital Ward. Day. EDITH *and* TOMMY *walking along it, past various beds, to a bed near the end, screened off. There is a NURSE with them. The NURSE pulls back the screen and cut from TOMMY's face and EDITH's face to a MAN, sitting up, grinning, his arm in a sling, having his pyjamas changed, and cut to:*
TOMMY *and* EDITH *walking on to the next bed, screened. The nurse opens the screen for them, and cut to GERALD's face on the pillow, eyes open, breath very faint, then:*
EDITH *is sitting in a chair beside him. TOMMY standing beside her. He looks down at GERALD's face, he makes a sound, turns his face away, clutches at EDITH's hand, and on the tableau:*

104. Interior. Kitchen. Day. TOMMY *and* EDITH *sitting at the table, a cup being raised to TOMMY's lips.*

EDITH (*almost desultory*). That's your fifth cup. You'll be ill.

TOMMY (*after a pause*). Four, I've only had four cups.

EDITH. That's still too many.

Little silence, as –

MRS MERCHANT *comes into the kitchen, walking on tip-toe. She stops by EDITH, looks down at her compassionately.*

(*Wanly smiling.*) I'll be all right. Really. Tommy's going to look after me, for a little.

MRS MERCHANT *gingerly touches EDITH's arm, she goes out. There is a silence.*

EDITH. You had two cups in that ghastly room, and two in the hospital canteen. It's your fifth.

TOMMY (*thinks, nods*). Fifth. (*Little silence.*) I won't have any more.

EDITH. What are you going to do now? Are you going to stay here?

After a pause, TOMMY *nods.*

I won't want you here.

TOMMY. I know.

EDITH. But you'll stay anyway?

TOMMY. Yes I will, Edie. I don't mind being inferior, see. I don't mind.

EDITH *looks at him, with a weary smile.*

EDITH. I shall despise you.

TOMMY. Sometimes. Other times you won't notice me, even. And I'll be nice to Giles. (*Little pause.*) I have no shame.

EDITH. No. That's your strength, isn't it?

TOMMY. Of course people will despise you for living with me.

EDITH. I'm quite strong too. (*She gets up, goes out of the kitchen.*)

105. Interior. Edith's Study. Day. *She enters, turns on the light, goes to the window, looks out. Suddenly she crosses herself, closing her eyes and lowering her head. She smiles ironically, turns to the desk.*
On the desk are the exercise books, neatly piled, and as the camera comes in on them:
Sounds of great chords of religious music, organ, which goes on as EDITH *approaches the desk slowly, as if in a trance, picks them up as if holding something sacred, turns around, her eyes aglow. The music still going on, solemn and magnificent, and:*

TOMMY (*at the door*). So he put them back then?

The music stops. There is a silence.

EDITH. You see. You see. I was bound to get them back. I'm a novelist. (*In a whisper.*) That's all I am. That's all I want to be.

I shall go on writing novels until I die. If God is good to me, I shall die as I finish a sentence. His Will Be Done.

Cut to:

TOMMY's *face, staring at her,* stay on his face *as organ music, over, starts again, gently,* mixing into EDITH *at her desk.*

106. Exterior. Garden. Day. *The organ music going on, as through the window to her side we see* MRS MERCHANT *in a deck chair, holding* GILES *in her arms, in an accidentally religious posture, and kneeling beside her,* TOMMY, *beside whom is a small jug of soapy water. He has his hands to his face, as if in prayer, blowing a mighty bubble.*
This shot freezes into a still, *as the organ music continues, and:*

Titles superimposed.

Fade out.

The End.